LUCY
(TAMMY)
CORWIN

the COVENANT

a study of God's extraordinary love for you

the COVENANT

a study of God's extraordinary love for you

JAMES L. GARLOW

BEACON HILL PRESS
OF KANSAS CITY

Copyright 1999, 2007
by Beacon Hill Press of Kansas City

First edition 1999
Second edition 2007

ISBN 978-0-8341-2329-8

Printed in the
United States of America

Cover Design: Chad A Cherry

Library of Congress Cataloging-in-Publication Data

Garlow, James L.
    The covenant : a Bible study / James L. Garlow.
        p.   cm.
    Originally published: Kansas City, Mo. : Beacon Hill Press of Kansas City, c1999.
    Includes bibliographical references.
    ISBN-13: 978-0-8341-2329-8 (pbk.)
    ISBN-10: 0-8341-2329-0 (pbk.)
  1. Covenants—Biblical teaching.   2. Covenants—Religious aspects—Christianity.   I. Title.

    BS680.C67G37   2007
    231.7'6—dc22   2007024168

10 9 8 7 6 5 4 3 2 1

This book is lovingly dedicated to the
one who has so graciously and
unselfishly shared the marriage covenant
with me since January 1971—
my wife, friend, lover, confidante,
and covenant partner—Carol

JIM GARLOW has served since 1995 as senior pastor of Skyline Wesleyan Church near San Diego, a dynamic congregation with a worship attendance of approximately 3,500. Prior to his move to California, he planted the Metroplex Chapel Church of the Nazarene in the Dallas-Fort Worth area in 1983, an innovative ministry that grew to over 800 in average attendance during his time there. He is the author of *How God Saved Civilization* (Regal Books) and *Partners in Ministry* (Beacon Hill Press of Kansas City). He serves on the Beeson Clergy Council of Asbury Theological Seminary and the advisory boards of Bartlesville Wesleyan College and *Ministries Today* magazine. Dr. Garlow holds degrees from Southern Nazarene University, Asbury Theological Seminary, Princeton Theological Seminary, and Drew University. He and his wife, Carol, are the parents of four children and one grandchild.

CONTENTS

ACKNOWLEDGMENTS

My sincere thanks to the following individuals:

My father, Burtis Garlow (1915-98), who by both word and example "lived the covenant" and who encouraged me to write.

My mother, Winifred Garlow, who also "lived the covenant" and who painstakingly typed my dictations and illegible scribbles.

I express heartfelt thanks also to the following persons, who each taught me a "piece" of the covenant:

Milton Green of In the Word Ministries, who called himself "a Southern Baptist carpet cleaner from Cleveland, Tennessee" and came to Dallas and touched us all.

Mike Haley, who wrote an article on the covenant for *Fulness* magazine while pastoring a Baptist church in Oklahoma.

Paul Billheimer, who wrote *Destined for the Throne,* one of the most provocative books I've ever read.

Charles Capps, a cotton farmer from the town of England, Arkansas, who taught me about our authority in Christ.

Kent Anderson, who in one sentence triggered my understanding of the major step in the covenant-making ceremony.

Henry Poteet, who in his late 80s has superb scriptural recall and is always willing to have another theological discussion about the covenant.

Malcolm Shelton, my professor at Southern Nazarene University who, even though I didn't understand it at the time, kept emphasizing that spectacular concept called "the covenant."

John Oswalt, my professor at Asbury Theological Seminary, who infected me with a passion for the Old Testament.

Lefferts Loetscher, my professor at Princeton Theological Seminary, who created in me an awareness of covenant theology.

1

so why is the COVENANT *so important?*

∞

"Life-changing" is a very strong term. We pastors are inclined to use it too often, such as when we sometimes promise that hearing a special speaker will be a life-changing experience. But this isn't always the case; not everything that is reported to be life-changing really is.

However, the story of the covenant is an exception. Here I use the term "life-changing" carefully and guardedly, for what you will read concerning the covenant will alter your thinking and significantly alter your life.

learning about the covenant

It was a cold December day in Dallas in 1983 when I made my way across the city to a hotel in the northern section of town. I had no reason to suspect that my life was about to be changed. The speaker for this three-day seminar was a man named Milton Green, who came with rather unusual credentials. He liked to refer to himself as "a Southern Baptist carpet cleaner from Cleveland, Tennessee." He opened the seminar by talking about the covenant.

I had heard the word "covenant" before. I remember Professor Malcolm Shelton talking about it when I was a graduate student at Southern Nazarene University in Bethany, Oklahoma. I recall hearing John Oswalt refer to it frequently when I was in the master of divinity program at Asbury Theological Seminary in Wilmore, Kentucky. I recall Lefferts Loetscher from Princeton Theological Seminary in New Jersey referring to covenant theology in early America. All of them were superb teachers, but apparently I was not a very attentive student. Somehow I never quite grasped the teaching on covenant.

But this day would be different. Milton Green began to describe the steps of the covenant-making ceremony. He spent only a short time on it, perhaps 20 or 30 minutes, but it launched me on a pursuit that has lasted for years. As he started through the steps, it was as if scales fell off my eyes. I turned to my pastor friend Travis, who was sitting beside me, and asked, "Have you ever heard this before?" He said he had not. When Milton began referring to the (new covenant,) my heart was pounding in anticipation. This was truly something new.

As a result, I began to study the covenant with intensity. I searched the Scriptures over and over—and for the first time in my life I wore the cover right off my Bible. Over the course of the next decade I would have numerous dialogues with my friend Pastor Henry Poteet, asking him repeatedly what he knew about this concept called the covenant. I preached on that topic in city after city, and each time I saw lives changed. It was the first time I had ever witnessed such a dramatic change of that sort. The covenant was impacting others the same way it had me.

the covenant is foundational

So why was this happening? What is it about the covenant

that is so life changing? From my studies I discovered some remarkable insights. For one thing, understanding the steps of the covenant-making ceremony and its role in human history causes many Bible verses to spring to life with meanings that may not have been previously considered. Looking closer, I found that in many ways the covenant is the foundation of our faith and the epicenter of what we understand about our relationship with God. Upon it is based our understanding of salvation, holiness, healing, worship, deliverance, and sanctification. The covenant is truly foundational, and discovering this can be exhilarating—even life changing.

early teaching on the covenant

Despite all its importance, not many books are written about the covenant. To find out why this is so, we need to go back in history, starting with June 16-18, 1885. On these dates a professor by the name of H. Clay Trumbull was asked to give a series of lectures. He chose to lecture on a topic that would eventually find its way into a book titled *The Blood Covenant: A Primitive Rite and Its Bearings on Scripture.* So positive was the response to this book that a second edition, with much added material, was released in January 1893. The book is a classic, for it opens new ground in understanding the depth of God's love for us and the way it has been articulated in the pages of Scripture.

In the years that would follow the second edition of Dr. Trumbull's writings, numerous writers would attempt to put it in popular form, some more successfully than others. Unfortunately, the basic message of his book has fallen by the wayside, and the term "covenant" is not generally understood by most of the people who benefit from its inexplicable privileges and promises.

what is a covenant?

The word "covenant" in its Hebrew form is used nearly 300 times in the Bible and comes from the root word meaning "to cut." In its simplest form, a covenant is an all-encompassing agreement between two parties with clearly outlined perimeters and promises. It is a mutual understanding between two persons who bind themselves together with specific obligations to fulfill. What's so significant about that? Why would I be so excited to share this concept with you when it involves such a simple definition?

when God initiated the covenant

The best way to find out why the covenant is so important is to take a look at what God had in mind from the start. The story of the covenant begins with God's heart being broken when He saw the destitution and destruction of humanity. He never designed His creation to be in such disarray and chaos. As He looked from heaven to earth, He observed that the ancient people (the people in Abram's time—2,000 years before Christ) participated in covenant-making ceremonies. They did this with full knowledge that once having committed themselves to each other, everything they had belonged to each other. They intentionally would release their individual identities in order to have a merged identity.

God knew that the covenant would be an effective way to reach humanity and help them understand the intensity of His love for them. By making a covenant with humanity, God would bind himself to them and ask them to bind themselves to Him. Doing this would mean that everything He had would belong to them—all the blessings of heaven would be theirs.

So God searched for a person, just one person, who might

The word "covenant" in its

Hebrew form is used nearly

300 times in the Bible. It

comes from the root word

meaning "to cut."

be capable of hearing from God and obeying Him so that He could establish this covenant relationship with him. Before long He discovered a young man named Abram, and He began to talk to him. At first the message seemed strange: "Leave your home. Go to a new place. I'm going to give you some land." Abram must have been puzzled, but God didn't give up. "I am going to enter into a relationship with you," He said.

"What kind of relationship?" Abram asked.

"The covenant," said God, assertively.

"The covenant?" queried Abram.

"Yes," said God.

"But, God—when people enter into covenant, it means that everything they have belongs to each other. Are You saying that You, Almighty God, would enter into a relationship with a mere human like me?"

"That is precisely My intention," replied God. And the covenant was born.

From a conversation something like this was launched the most profound, compelling scriptural truth of all human history. For the covenant that God made was not merely with Abram (Abraham); it was with all his spiritual descendants. That's you and me.

Then Why Haven't We Heard About This Before?

Again, we return to the question of why something as important as the covenant is rarely mentioned except in casual reference. Why haven't we heard sermons about it? Why haven't we read books and listened to tapes or CDs about it? Why doesn't the Bible refer to it more and explain it better?

Dr. Trumbull in his late 19th-century classic work deals very well with that specific issue: (It seems strange that a primitive rite like the Blood Covenant, with its world-wide sweep, and its manifold applications to the history of sacrifice, should have received so little attention. . . . The suggestion of any real importance in the religious symbolism of this rite has been generally brushed aside without its receiving due consideration."[2])

But there is an even further explanation as to why it is not thoroughly explained in the Bible itself. Simply stated,("Because the primitive rite of Blood Covenanting was *well-known* in the Lands of the Bible, at the time of the writing of the Bible, for that very reason we are not to look to the Bible for specific explanations of the rite itself, even where there are incidental references in the Bible to the rite and its observances; but, on the other hand, we are to find an explanation of the biblical illustrations of the primitive rite, in the understanding of that rite which we gain from outside sources. In this way, we are able to see in the Bible much that otherwise would be lost sight of."[3]

In other words, the Bible doesn't need to give a thorough explanation of the covenant, because the people in that time simply understood its significance and importance. We have a distinct *dis*advantage. So many of us today read the Bible as Westerners, not Easterners, and from a vantage point several thousand years later.(We don't have covenant-making ceremonies in our culture (with a single exception of the wedding ceremony), thus we have no way to relate to this remarkable event and its profound implications in demonstrating the intensity of God's love and passion for us.)

multiple covenants

(The covenant that we will be focusing on in this book is referred to as the Abrahamic covenant, with its implications for the new covenant of Christ.)Sometimes it is referred to as the "blood covenant."(But this is not the only covenant found in

Scripture. Multiple times God reached down and made a unique agreement with humanity. We will not examine the other covenants in this book;[4] we will merely list them.

The first was the Edenic covenant, found in Gen. 1:26-30. This agreement involved God and Adam and some specific requirements and promises. The second was the Adamic covenant, coming from the name Adam, in Gen. 3:1-24 and involved God's agreement with Adam after sin entered the human race. The third was the Noahic covenant, in Gen. 8 and 9, in which God made an agreement with Noah that literally started the human race over again. The fourth was the Abrahamic covenant, the blood covenant, which will be the major focus of this book. The fifth was the Mosaic covenant, found in Exod. 20 and 40, and involved some specific agreements between God and the children of Israel. The sixth was the Davidic covenant, from the time of David, as found in 2 Sam. 7 and Ps. 89. The seventh and last is the new covenant, referenced in Matt. 26:28. In the chapters to follow we will observe the profound linkage between the Abrahamic covenant and the exciting new covenant.

so why should we be so excited about the covenant?

Why is "covenant" such a significant term? It is simply this: "Covenant" is a word that describes God's relationship to you and me. Since the very creation of the world, God had used a unique pattern, a unique cultural event, referred to as the covenant. Through this He outlined specific requirements and spectacular promises and tells us how He wants us to respond to Him, outlining the promises of what will happen if we follow His ways. And those promises are absolutely thrilling—even life changing, as I hope you will discover in the next few pages.

review and reflect

1. What is a covenant?

2. Why would God choose the covenant-making ceremony as a way of reaching out to us?

3. Why does the Bible not give specific explanations for the rites in the covenant ceremony?

2

the powerful
old COVENANT

∞

Sometime after God called Abram to follow Him, the two were conversing. God reminded Abram of the original promise of the land. Abram wondered how he could be certain that God would come through with His part of the deal. God said, "Get a heifer." Abram's heart pounded with excitement. He knew what God meant—the contract was about to be signed.

"And He said to him, 'I am the LORD who brought you out of Ur of the Chaldeans, to give you this land to possess it.' He said, 'O Lord GOD, how may I know that I will possess it?' So He said to him, 'Bring Me a three year old heifer, and a three year old female goat, and a three year old ram, and a turtledove, and a young pigeon.' Then he brought all these to Him and cut them in two, and laid each half opposite the other; but he did not cut the birds. The birds of prey came down upon the carcasses, and Abram drove them away. Now when the sun was going down, a deep sleep fell upon Abram; and behold, terror and great darkness fell upon him" (Gen. 15:7-12).

"It came about when the sun had set, that it was very dark, and behold, there appeared a smoking oven and a flaming torch which passed between these pieces. On that day the LORD made a covenant with Abram, saying, 'To your descendants I have given this land'" (vv. 17-18).

In the above scriptures, God gave Abram some very unusual instructions. Abram had recently left Ur of the Chaldeans, his home country, to follow God to this uncharted territory. God had promised him real estate, and Abram was expectant.

"I'm here, God," he said, "ready for all You promised me."

"Go get a heifer," God answered. This reply was no surprise to Abram. Sacrificing a heifer was the language of contracts in those days. With those words, Abram knew he was about to make a contract with God.

In the ancient Middle Eastern world a practice called "making covenant," or "cutting covenant," was common. A covenant was an all-encompassing agreement between two parties. The closest comparison to it in our modern culture is marriage. But with the current prevalence of divorce, even marriage doesn't compare. Once a person entered into a covenant in the ancient Middle Eastern world, specifically the blood covenant, he or she could not be released from it.

In the culture of Abram it was common for tribal chiefs or heads of city-states to enter into covenants or alliances with one another. So when God wanted to communicate to humanity, He used the covenant, because it was a vehicle people would immediately understand. After the fall of Adam and Eve and at the time of Abram, creation had gone awry. Making covenant would be a way God could demonstrate His love for humanity and His deep desire to have fellowship with individuals. Entering into covenant was a language that pagan cultures would understand. The Old Testament of the Bible is called the "old covenant"; the New Testament is called the "new covenant."

The covenant-making ceremony was an agreement between two people. It involved several steps that were completed publicly in an open field before a crowd of witnesses.[1]

exchange of robes

Step one of the covenant-making ceremony was the exchange of robes; this represented an exchange of identity. The two parties would take their outer garments and exchange them. If someone saw one of the partners from a distance, he or she might say, "Here comes Jim Garlow. But wait—he doesn't walk like Jim; he's not built like Jim. But isn't that Jim's robe he's wearing?" The exchange of robes represents a confusion of identity.

exchange of belts

The second step was the exchange of belts. This represented an exchange of strength. The covenant partners traded belts. These belts were larger than we wear today and were the place from which military gear was hung. Exchanging them symbolized the sharing of strengths or assets. If we exchanged belts, my covenant partner would be saying to me, "Jim, everything I bring to this relationship is now yours. And everything you have is now mine. Our strengths and our assets are now combined."

exchange of weapons

The third step in the covenant-making ceremony was the exchange of weapons that hung on the belt. This symbolized an exchange of enemies and declared that the covenant partners would protect each other from harm.

sacrifice

The fourth step was the sacrifice of an animal or several animals. The animal must be cut.[2] Normally a heifer would be laid on its back and sliced down the underside of its belly. Its legs would then be folded out. The sacrifice of the animal is why we term this kind of covenant the *blood* covenant. As mentioned in the previous chapter, there were other covenants as well: the Adamic covenant, the Edenic covenant, and the Noahic covenant, to name a few. But the Abrahamic covenant is the most significant to believers today. It is the blood covenant. And every time a blood covenant was made, a sacrifice was needed. Life must be given, and blood must be shed. When God asked Abram to get a heifer, Abram did *not* say, "A heifer? I wanted a contract! What about my land You promised?" Abram knew that the heifer *was* a contract—in fact, it was an *irrevocable* contract.

walk of death

The fifth step was the walk of death. At this point in the ceremony, the covenant partners stood facing each other in an open field. The animal lay cut open between them. The partners literally walked through the mass of blood. One would walk through and come back on the left side. The other would come back through, turning toward the right. Together they patterned a figure eight.[3]

mark on the body

The sixth step in the covenant-making ceremony was a mark placed on the body. In the old culture, it was the "striking of hands." In the Hebrew culture the hand includes what we would call the wrist. The covenant partners made an incision on their wrists, and the two would then put their wrists together, mingling their blood in what is called "the striking of hands." Some primitive cultures still practice this, taking an abrasive substance like gunpowder and rubbing it in to darken the area under the skin and make the wound more pronounced so that there is a permanent mark on the body.[4] Some traditions say that the modern custom of waving our hand in greeting originates from the practice of raising hands in such a way to reveal the covenant mark. By doing so, one person let another know that he or she had a covenant partner. This suggests that the origin of the handclasp, as in the shaking of hands, comes from the cutting of a covenant.[5] The two individuals would clasp hands as the blood from their freshly cut wrists flowed together. The covenant mark on the wrists or palms might be what is referred to in Isa. 49:16, in which God states, "I have inscribed you on the palms of My hands."

pronouncement of blessings and curses

The seventh step in covenant making was the pronouncements of blessings and curses. This occurred in the presence of the witnesses after cutting the heifer, walking through the pieces, and striking the hands. At this point in the ceremony, the partners faced one another, and each said these words: "So long as you keep the terms of this covenant, blessed shall you be when you go out and when you come in. Blessed shall you be when you rise up and when you lay down. Blessed shall be your wife, blessed shall be your children, blessed shall be all that you put your hands to." Because the culture revolved around an agrarian or agricultural economy, he would say, "Blessed shall be your oxen, your donkeys, your fields, and the produce of your fields." After a pause, he would continue: "But if you violate the terms of this covenant, cursed shall you be when you rise up and lay down. Cursed shall be your wife, your children. Cursed shall be your oxen, your donkeys, your land." And on and on he would go. When he had ended, his partner would pronounce the same blessings and curses. These pronouncements signified that two people were entering into oneness.

covenant meal

The eighth step was the covenant meal. The covenant partners sat at a table before the witnesses and shared a meal. But the partners didn't begin by feeding themselves. They fed each other the first few bites, saying, "As you are ingesting this food, you are ingesting me; you are taking me into your life." When a bride and a groom feed each other cake today, the act is symbolic of the covenant-making ceremony.

exchange of names

The ninth step in the covenant-making ceremony is the exchange of names. The partners once again stood facing each other in the open field. Let's suppose I was making a covenant with someone named Bob Smith. I would say, "Bob, in order to let my enemies know who my covenant partner is, I will take your name and put it in the middle of mine. No longer will I be known simply as Jim Garlow. From this moment I will be known as Jim *Smith* Garlow." And my covenant partner, Bob Smith, would say, "From this moment on, my name will be Bob *Garlow* Smith, so that every time my name is pronounced, it tells all the people who my covenant partner is."

This name change is precisely what occurred when God made covenant with Abram. The man's name changed from Abram to Abr*AH*am. The two letters that are added are "AH," which come from Yahwa (YAH-way),[6] the name of God that appears approximately 6,800 times in the Old Testament. We pronounce it "Jehovah." God doesn't stop there. True to covenant, He takes Abraham's name. From this point on, He calls himself "the God of Abraham."

In the Old Testament no one word adequately describes God. There are multiple names for Him, each of which depicts a feature or an aspect of His character. The one used in Gen. 15 is "Yahweh," which we commonly read as "Jehovah." "Yahweh" means "the oath-making God" or "the oath-keeping God." God is the original promise keeper. He is the covenant maker and the covenant keeper.

In ancient Hebrew there were no vowels—only consonants. The letter "a" in "Yahweh" is a pronunciation aid that was added later. But originally God's name was simply four letters: "YHWH." When He made covenant with Abram, He put the "H" from His name into Abraham's name and changed Sara's name to "Sarah." The Hebrew letter "H" is the sound of breath, generally signifying the breath or presence of God.[7]

In Gen. 1 we read about the creation of man and woman. When God made Adam from the dust, the first man was merely a body. What made Adam live? The breath of God. We see the same concept in the New Testament. The Holy Spirit is called the "Holy *Pneuma*" in Greek. *Pneuma* means wind; literally it means *the Holy puff of breath of God.* We can see the significance of the letter that symbolizes breath being put in the middle of Abram's name as a symbol that God is his covenant partner. Abram becomes Abr*AH*am. In fact, the relationship is so meaningful that the author of 2 Chronicles, when talking to God, calls Abraham "Your friend" (2 Chron. 20:7). God refers to him as "My friend" in Isa. 41:8, and James calls him "the friend of God" (James 2:23).

As we have seen, God also took Abraham's name. Throughout Scripture, time after time, He calls himself "the God of Abraham." Attached to God's title is the name of this man, His covenant partner.

The tenth step in covenant making is also a very important one. We will discuss it in a later chapter.

review and reflect

1. Briefly list the nine steps of the covenant-making ceremony discussed in this chapter, and summarize each one.

2. Why did God choose the covenant as a vehicle by which to communicate His love to us?

3. Why was the covenant made publicly?

4. What ceremony today most resembles the ancient rite of making covenant?

5. Describe your reaction to chapter 2, including any personal application you derived from your reading.

3

COVENANT *language in the old testament*

∞

There are many examples of covenant language in the Old Testament. For instance, Gen. 17:1 says, "Now when Abram was ninety-nine years old, the LORD appeared to Abram and said to him, 'I am God Almighty.'" Here is another name for God— "El-Shaddai," a hyphenated word. "El" means mighty or strong. "Shaddai" is derived from the word meaning "breast," which implies nurturing, as in caring for a young baby. So it means the God who is mighty, who is tender, who cares for me as a parent would care for a young child.[1] "I am God Almighty [El-Shaddai]; walk before Me, and be blameless," God says. Note that the admonition is not to be faultless, but *blameless.*

circumcision—the covenant mark on the body

The scripture continues, "No longer shall your name be called Abram, but your name shall be Abraham; for I will make you the father of a multitude of nations. I will make you exceedingly fruitful, and I will make nations of you, and kings will come forth from you. I will establish My covenant between Me and you and your descendants after you" (Gen. 17:5-7).

The covenant is *multigenerational,* going on generation after generation. Let's move to verses 10 and 11: "This is My covenant, which you shall keep, between Me and you and your descendants after you: every male among you shall be circumcised. And you shall be circumcised in the flesh of your foreskin, and it shall be the sign of the covenant between Me and you."

In contemporary culture we may be uncomfortable discussing something as delicate as circumcision. However, circumcision was extremely significant in the Old Testament, because it represented covenant. It was the mark on a man's body that signified that he was in covenant with Someone else. We saw the importance of a mark on the body in step six of the covenant ceremony. In this Scripture passage the male reproductive organ represents the capacity to procreate. Unlike today, when many persons consider children merely an inconvenience, in Old Testament times they were the greatest asset a man could have. The greatest curse that could befall a woman was barrenness. In light of this paradigm, God declared that on the part of a man's body that brings him the greatest pleasure and his most important blessing would be a mark indicating a covenant relationship.

"You and I are in covenant," He was saying, "and everything you have, including your children, is mine." This is covenant language.

blessings

We see covenant language again in Deut. 28, which includes the pronouncement of blessings and curses we saw in step seven of the covenant ceremony. "Now it shall be, if you diligently obey the LORD your God, being careful to do all His command-

Biblical prosperity is God's

desire to meet our needs

without our experiencing

undue stress.

ments which I command you today, the LORD your God will set you high above all the nations of the earth. All these blessings will come upon you and overtake you if you obey the LORD your God" (vv. 1-2). Verses 3-4 and 6-7 continue: "Blessed shall you be in the city, and blessed shall you be in the country. Blessed shall be the offspring of your body and the produce of your ground and the offspring of your beasts, the increase of your herd and the young of your flock. . . . Blessed shall you be when you come in, and blessed shall you be when you go out. The LORD shall cause your enemies who rise up against you to be defeated before you; they will come out against you one way and will flee before you seven ways." When your enemies come to tamper with you, let them know who your covenant partner is. One of the blessings inherent in the covenant relationship is that we are partners with powerful and fearsome Almighty God.

prosperity

The covenant language continues in verse 11: "The LORD will make you abound in prosperity." Prosperity is a biblical concept. Although some have distorted this doctrine to mean nothing more than big cars and fancy houses, prosperity is a powerful theme in Scripture. Biblical prosperity is God's desire to meet our needs without our experiencing undue stress. He desires to bless us in the same way any good earthly father wants to take care of his children:

> The LORD will make you abound in prosperity, in the offspring of your body and in the offspring of your beast and in the produce of your ground, in the land which the LORD swore to your fathers to give you. The LORD will open for you His good storehouse, the heavens, to give rain to your land in its season and to bless all the work of your hand; and you shall lend to many nations, but you shall not

borrow. The LORD will make you the head and not the tail, and you only will be above, and you will not be underneath, if you will listen to the commandments of the LORD your God *(Deut. 28:11-13)*.

curses

The pronouncement of blessings is followed by the pronouncement of curses, a continuation of covenant language:

> But it shall come about, if you do not obey the LORD your God, to observe to do all His commandments and His statutes with which I charge you today, that all these curses will come upon you and overtake you: Cursed shall you be in the city, and cursed shall you be in the country. Cursed shall be your basket and your kneading bowl. Cursed shall be the offspring of your body and the produce of your ground, the increase of your herd and the young of your flock. Cursed shall you be when you come in, and cursed shall you be when you go out. The LORD will send upon you curses, confusion, and rebuke, in all you undertake to do, until you are destroyed and until you perish quickly, on account of the evil of your deeds. . . . The LORD will smite you with consumption *(Deut. 28:15-20, 22)*.

the enemy—robber of God's blessings

The curses continue: "The heaven which is over your head shall be bronze. . . . The LORD shall cause you to be defeated before your enemies. . . . Your carcasses will be food to all birds of the sky and to the beasts of the earth, and *there will be no one to frighten them away*"(Deut. 28:23, 25-26, emphasis added).

This passage is not the only time the Bible speaks of birds in a similar context. Two chapters in Jeremiah, 7 and 34, are good examples. Note the covenant language in the following passage: "I will give the men who have transgressed My *covenant,* who have not fulfilled the words of the *covenant* which they made before Me, when they *cut the calf in two and passed between its parts* . . . I will give them into the hand of their enemies and into the hand of those who seek their life. And their dead bodies will be food for the birds of the sky and the beasts of the earth" (Jer. 34:18, 20, emphasis added).

Jer. 7:33 is another place in which birds are referenced: "The dead bodies of this people will be food for the birds of the sky and for the beasts of the earth; and *no one will frighten them away"* (emphasis added). You'll recall that we also read about birds in Gen. 15:11 when *Abram frightened them away* after cutting the animal in the covenant ceremony.

What does all this talk about birds mean? We find a clue in a New Testament parable about soils. The sower, Jesus says in Mark 4, went out to sow the seed, and it fell on four different types of ground. Some of it landed on rocky soil, and the birds took it and carried it away (Mark 4:4).

Jesus interprets His remarks later in the chapter. The birds represent the enemy, He says, robbing the Word before it has a chance to take root in a believer's life (Mark 4:15). We see that even as far back as the covenant-making ceremony in Gen. 15, God's touch does something profound and significant in a person's life. When we plant the Word of God down deep inside us, a transformation takes place. Jesus is telling us that there are always birds of prey (the enemy) trying to pluck the seed God has planted before it can take root, before it can begin to grow, and before it can produce a harvest. *Whenever God does something profound in our hearts, the enemy shows up to try to diminish its impact in our lives.* Abram was in the midst of making covenant with God when the birds of prey swooped down to

Whenever God does

something profound in our

hearts, the enemy shows up

to try to diminish its

impact in our lives.

steal the spoils. Knowing the nature of the enemy, Abram shooed them away with authority. That is precisely what we as believers must learn to do. *Whenever God gives us a new insight or establishes something deep within our spirits, we must learn to protect ourselves before the enemy robs us of that experience with God.*

david and goliath—the test of the covenant

Let's follow a story in 1 Samuel, paying close attention to what we can learn about the covenant and covenant language in Scripture. The story of David and Goliath begins in 1 Sam. 17:3—"The Philistines stood on the mountain on one side while Israel stood on the mountain on the other side, with the valley between them. Then a champion came out from the armies of the Philistines named Goliath, from Gath, whose height was six cubits and a span" (vv. 3-4). (A cubit is a measurement from the elbow to the tip of the finger and is roughly 18 inches. It means he stood about 9 or 10 feet tall.)

What is happening in this story? Goliath is on one side of the valley. On the other side stands Saul, the great warrior-king. With him are his army personnel and David's older brothers. David, a boy who attends his father's sheep, has just arrived because his father sent him over with food for his brothers. As David approaches, he finds the group of men standing together commiserating about their plight. "No, we can't take on Goliath," they agree.

At this point David speaks up: "What will you do for me if I go get this guy?" he asks. Let's pick up the story at verse 26: "David spoke to the men who were standing by him, saying, 'What will be done for the man who kills this Philistine and takes away the reproach from Israel? For who is this *uncircum-*

cised Philistine, that he should taunt the armies of the living God?'" (emphasis added). When David mentions circumcision, he is not talking about anatomy—he is talking about covenant. David is really saying something like this: "Who is this out-of-covenant person that he should mess with us? It makes no difference if he is 9 or 10 feet tall. It makes no difference if I'm a shepherd boy. He is *out* of covenant. I am *in* covenant, and my covenant partner is God. Let's go."

In verse 33, Saul protests David's youthful naïveté: "You're just a youth. What do you know about fighting a war, kid?"

But David knows his covenant theology. In verses 34-35 he says, "Your servant was tending his father's sheep. When a lion or a bear came and took a lamb from the flock, I went out after him and attacked him, and rescued it from his mouth; and when he rose up against me, I seized him by his beard and struck him and killed him."

"Your servant has killed both the lion and the bear; and this uncircumcised Philistine will be like one of them, since he has taunted the armies of the living God" (v. 36). That is, he has taunted the covenant partners of God.

David continues to speak in covenant language: "The LORD who delivered me from the paw of the lion and from the paw of the bear, He will deliver me from the hand of this Philistine" (v. 37). Interestingly, Saul buys into David's argument, but only for putting David in the line of danger, not himself.

"OK, David," Saul says. "Go ahead." And although Saul doesn't offer to go fight himself (he's a covenant partner too), he offers to let David use his armor. Verses 38-39 tell us, "Then Saul clothed David with his garments and put a bronze helmet on his head, and he clothed him with armor. David girded his sword over his armor and tried to walk."

Saul's sword is so big for the lanky David that it simply

Instead, we cling to our

programs and promotions,

admiring our cleverness

and hoping God will bless

it. Like Saul, we rely on

the flesh.

stakes him to the ground, causing him to spin in circles. One translation says, "He tried in vain to walk" (v. 39, NRSV). Simply put, Saul's armor is too big, and David is too small.

the church today

Here stands David now with a sword that's too big for him to carry. The mental imagery reminds me of the contemporary Church. We, like Saul, sing songs of bravado. We're "covenant kids." But then we load ourselves with all kinds of "weapons" —programs, productions, and promotions instead of prayer, power, praise, and purity.

Programs, productions, and promotions are not wrong if they are birthed from the heart of God. But in our human ingenuity we sometimes say, "I'm going to build this thing." When we finish we say, "OK now, God—bless this mess." Perhaps we would be wiser to say, "God, please give me Your ideas, because *Your* plans are *already* anointed." Instead, we cling to our programs and promotions, admiring our cleverness and hoping God will bless it. Like Saul, we rely on the flesh.

(David knows his confidence is not in the flesh.) He is prepared to go forth in covenant power: "That all this assembly may know that the LORD does not deliver by sword or by spear; for the battle is the LORD's and He will give you into our hands," he says in verse 47.

After striking Goliath with the stone, "David ran and stood over the Philistine and took his sword and drew it out of its sheath and killed him, and cut off his head with it" (v. 51). David won the victory not because he was bigger or better but because he walked in covenant.

God

david and jonathan making covenant

We learn more about covenant beginning in 1 Sam. 18:1: "Now it came about when he had finished speaking to Saul, that the soul of Jonathan was knit to the soul of David, and Jonathan loved him as himself." The covenant Jonathan makes with David is described beginning in verse 4: "Jonathan stripped himself of the robe that was on him and gave it to David"—this is step number one in the covenant-making ceremony, the exchange of identity—"with his armor, including his sword and his bow and his belt." The giving of his belt represented the exchange of strength; and the giving of his weapons signified the exchange of enemies. David and Jonathan thus become full-fledged covenant partners.

The story doesn't end here. In 2 Sam. 4:4 we find out that several years later both Saul and Jonathan have been killed. They are survived by Jonathan's crippled five-year-old son Mephibosheth, who was injured when his nurse tried to smuggle him out of danger upon learning that Dad and Grandpa were dead.

Let's pick up the story again in 2 Sam. 9. It is many years later. David, now the king, is lonesome for his covenant partner Jonathan. Allow me to take some poetic license here by speculating that David and Jonathan had made the mark on the wrist (the striking of hands) when they made covenant. Perhaps the alleged covenant mark David bore on his wrist served to remind him frequently of his loss of Jonathan.

"Is there yet anyone left of the house of Saul, that I may show him kindness for Jonathan's sake?" David asks in verse 1. The word "kindness" actually is the word *chesed* in the Hebrew, which implies a tenacious love that will not give up. It's covenant love. I prefer to call it "pit bull love," because it never lets go. It's the "O Love That Will Not Let Me Go"* type of love. Even after all these years, he misses Jonathan desperately. A house servant named Ziba tells the king about Mephibosheth, who was living in a place called Lo-debar. The boy is crippled in both feet. King David instructs his servant Ziba to go find Jonathan's son.

Mephibosheth is convinced the meeting is not a good idea. Perhaps David thinks that because he is Saul's descendant, he wants to lead an insurrection. Perhaps David will kill him.

Verse 6 tells us, "Mephibosheth, the son of Jonathan the son of Saul, came to David and fell on his face and prostrated himself. And David said, 'Mephibosheth.' And he said, 'Here is your servant!'"

Instead of the wrath he expects, Mephibosheth finds mercy and a houseful of blessing. We can imagine David looking down at the covenant mark that was possibly on his wrist and showing it to Mephibosheth as he reaches out to his beloved friend's son.

And David says to him, "Do not fear, for I will surely show kindness [*chesed*] to you for the sake of your father Jonathan, and will restore to you all the land of your grandfather Saul; and you shall eat at my table regularly" (v. 7). (The NKJV says, "You shall eat bread at my table continually." I would rather eat "continually" than "regularly," wouldn't you?)

Mephibosheth does not understand David's kindness. It is more extravagant than he can comprehend. "Again he prostrated himself and said, 'What is your servant, that you should regard a dead dog like me?'" (v. 8). Mephibosheth sees himself as someone contemptible and does not understand the covenant. But as time would pass, he would understand its implication.

---

*Title of hymn written by George Matheson (1842—1906).

From that time on, Mephibosheth would eat at David's table as one of the king's sons.

Jesus, you, and me

This historical event has incredible spiritual application. You and I are tucked away in this story. The narrative is a picture of something spectacular: David represents Jesus; Ziba represents the Holy Spirit. Mephibosheth, whose name means "despised one" or "one who struggles with Baal," represents us. And "Lo-debar" means "a dry and parched land" where we live spiritually. It was a place of deprivation, a place of death, a place of fear. Literally, it means "the land of no word," a land where people had been deprived of teaching on the covenant, a land where truth does not prevail.

You see, David does for Mephibosheth what Jesus does for us. A crippled man, dwelling in a lonely and desolate place, doesn't know the truth of who he is—the son of a covenant partner. So David sends Ziba to get Mephibosheth—just as God sends the Holy Spirit to pursue us and bring us to Jesus.

Mephibosheth represents us. Jesus looks at the covenant mark, where the nails pierced His wrist, and says, "Are there any more offspring out there who have not known the benefits of the covenant? Invite them to My banquet table—compel them to come! Ziba, [Holy Spirit], go get them and bring them home."

Like Mephibosheth, our response to God's offer is often mixed. We know we are unworthy, emotionally crippled, living in a spiritually deprived land. So we fall on our face, imploring, "Don't kill me, Lord!"

"No, no," Jesus replies. "You're not here to be punished. The price has been paid! I bear the proof of the covenant mark. Leave Lo-debar behind! You are here to share My banquet table. It's spread for you. According to covenant, *what's Mine is yours.*"

The sad truth is that the Church (that's us) often lives below the covenant provision God intended.

This phrase is the most awesome aspect of the covenant. Jesus says in all sincerity and love, (*What's Mine is yours.*)

The glorious truth of the gospel is that God has given us His riches in Christ Jesus. He never intended for us to be "despised," and living in desolation. (The sad truth is that the Church (that's us) often lives below the covenant provision God intended.) what's rich?

Understanding the covenant and the covenant language in the Bible is foundational to the Christian life. By virtue of the covenant, all of heaven's resources are available to you. Everything that Jesus is and Jesus has is available to you as a covenant partner with Him today.

review and reflect

1. Describe the significance of birds in the Old and New Testaments.

2. What Goliaths are you facing in your life? How could David's approach apply to your situation?

3. How do we rely on Saul's armor today?

4. In what way are you crippled like Mephibosheth?

5. In what way is Ziba seeking you out?

6. What is Jesus doing now to show you the covenant marks on His wrist?

7. Are you living in Lo-debar or in the king's palace?

4

the even-more-powerful
new COVENANT

∞

Let's walk through the covenant-making ceremony again but from a new and *better* perspective. You see, the new covenant is better than the old covenant.

Look at Heb. 7:22 and 8:6: "So much the more also Jesus has become the guarantee of a better covenant. . . . But now He has obtained a more excellent ministry, by as much as He is also the mediator of a better covenant, which has been enacted on better promises."

In what way are the promises better? The answer to that is found in the word "atonement." We commonly use this word to describe what happened when Jesus died on the Cross: He *atoned* for our sin. We find the term in the Old Testament over 100 times. Surprisingly, in most translations of the *New* Testament the word "atonement" is not mentioned. The verb ("atone") means ("to cover." In the Old Testament sins were *covered*. But in the New Testament it is not a case of our sins being covered. What happens in the New Testament? Our sins are *wiped away*—they are *gone!* That's what the new covenant is all about.

If you grew up in a church, you might remember singing a song in Sunday School that went "Gone, gone, gone, gone! / Yes, my sins are gone."* At the time, it seemed like just a cute little children's song. In reality, it was a profound covenant theology.

There is another reason the promises of the new covenant make it superior to the old covenant. The old covenant is a *shadow* of the new covenant, which is "the real thing." Heb. 10:1 says, "The Law . . . has only a shadow of the good things to come and not the very form of things." By looking at a shadow I can tell a lot about an object, what the real thing might look like. But a shadow is only two-dimensional. My view becomes three-dimensional when I look at the object itself. And there is a great deal of difference between the two.

The Old Testament is a shadow of something yet to come. When we move to the New Testament, we are in a sense moving from two dimensions to three dimensions. In addition to that, Jesus is the Incarnation, God coming in human flesh—the real thing. We see this concept clearly in the *new* covenant-making ceremony.   Incarnation

exchange of robes

Envision this: When Jesus and I entered into covenant, we stood in an open field facing each other before a crowd of witnesses. In essence, Jesus said, "Tell you what, Jim—I'll exchange outer garments with you. I'll exchange robes."

I looked at my sport coat and then I looked at His. "Jesus," I said, "Your coat is brand-new, top-of-the-line, the best I've ever seen. Mine is tattered and threadbare. I'm ready to throw it away."

"I know," He said. "I'll swap you even."

That's exactly what we did. We swapped outer garments. Our identities were confused, and consequently here's what happened: the Father took a long look at me and saw that I was wrapped in robes of righteousness. "I like what I see," He said.

Then the Father looked down and saw His own Son, who was clothed in my robes of sinfulness. Jesus paid an extremely high price for swapping that outer garment. 2 Cor. 5:21 tells us, "He made Him who knew no sin to be sin on our behalf."

The significance of the exchange of robes can also be seen in Phil. 2:7-8. "[He] emptied Himself, taking the form of a bond-servant, and being made in the likeness of men. Being found in appearance as a man, He humbled Himself by becoming obedient to the point of death, even death on a cross." These verses are called the kenosis passage. Translated from the Greek, the concept is this: to empty oneself of oneself. You and I can't do that, but God can and did. Jesus wrapped himself in my robe of flesh, my robe of sinfulness. When the exchange of outer garments took place, I have, according to 2 Cor. 5:21, the righteousness of Christ. While everyone seems so concerned about "upward social mobility," Jesus chooses "*downward* social mobility" in order to identify with us.

exchange of belts

The second step in the covenant ceremony is the exchange of belts. When Jesus and I entered into covenant, we exchanged belts, which represents the exchange of strength. In 2 Cor. 12:7-10 Paul wrote, "Because of the surpassing greatness of the revelations, for this reason, to keep me from exalting myself, there was given me a thorn in the flesh, a messenger of Satan to torment me—to keep me from exalting myself! Concerning

Isa.

this I implored the Lord three times that it might leave me. And He has said to me, 'My grace is sufficient for you, for power is perfected in weakness.' Most gladly, therefore, I will rather boast about my weaknesses." This is covenant language. Notice the exchange taking place—"that the power of Christ may dwell in me. Therefore I am well content with weaknesses, with insults, with distresses, with persecutions, with difficulties, for Christ's sake; for when I am *weak,* then I am *strong*" (emphasis added). (The exchange of belts symbolizes the exchange of strengths or assets.)

The traditional interpretation of 2 Cor. 12:7 is that Paul's thorn in the flesh was a physical ailment, perhaps failing eyesight. The most bizarre interpretation I have ever heard is that it referred to his mother-in-law! I think there's a better interpretation. The term "thorn in the flesh" is a "Hebrewism," an idiom unique to the language. The phrase is used the same way we might say "the four corners of the earth." Of course, we don't believe the earth is flat and has corners, as people did centuries ago. We are speaking figuratively. We find similar phrases referring to a thorn three times in the Old Testament: Num. 33:55; Josh. 23:13; and Judg. 2:3 (see NIV). In all three cases it refers to ungodly people trying to stop the work of God. I believe that is precisely what is referred to in 2 Cor. 12:7. I propose that the thorn refers to ungodly (out-of-covenant) persons trying to block what God is doing through His covenant children.

According to 2 Cor. 12, Paul cried out to God three times asking Him to remove the thorn. He responded with a single phrase: "My grace is sufficient for you" (v. 9). Many persons have interpreted that to mean "Keep a stiff upper lip and hang in there, Paul. Just get through this one. It's going to be OK."

But that's not what God is saying. I believe He's saying, "Paul, if anybody ought to know about grace, it's you. You've walked

The firepower of the enemy

is no match for a believer

armed with covenant

authority.

with Me for years. You've proven Me time and time again. You understand resurrection power. Operate in My strength."

For Christians, the standard interpretation of grace has generally been "unmerited love." That's not an inaccurate definition, but it is an *inadequate* definition. Grace, biblically understood, is God's willingness to unleash His power in my behalf though I don't deserve it.

This concept is intriguing. Nowhere does the New Testament ever say, "When Satan attacks you, cry out to God, who will get back with you as soon as He gets time."

It's not as if we call God on His hot line with no results: "Hello, God—it's Jim. Yeah, Satan's on my back again. How soon can You be here? Fifteen minutes? OK. I'll just hang in there in the meantime."

On the contrary, the New Testament tells us to live with power and authority, *"[You] resist the devil and he will flee from you,"* says James 4:7. The firepower of the enemy is no match for a believer armed with covenant authority. We can bring down the strongholds of the devil. Our weapons are mighty. Believers have power because God is willing to unleash His power on our behalf.

Zech. 4 deals with this same truth. The Jewish people were assigned the task of rebuilding the Temple after it had been destroyed by invading armies, and Zerubbabel was their leader. To rebuild the Temple, the Israelites had to quarry rocks out of a great mountain.

In the midst of this seemingly impossible task, the Word of the Lord came to Zerubbabel saying, "Not by might nor by power, but by My Spirit" (v. 6). Verse 7 continues, "What are you, O great mountain? Before Zerubbabel you will become a plain; and he will bring forth the top stone with shouts of 'Grace, grace to it!'"

God is telling Zerubbabel to "speak grace" to a mountain. What does that mean? It means He's going to partner with you. "Together we'll bring this mountain down and make it a plain," God says.

In the New Testament we see mountains referred to again, this time as a Hebrew idiom. When Jesus tells us to "say to this mountain, 'Be taken up and cast into the sea'" (Matt. 21:21), He isn't referring to a literal mountain. All of us have mountains or difficulties we face in life, challenges and struggles. God is in the business of helping us bring down mountains and make them into plains.

Skyline Wesleyan Church in San Diego, the church I pastor, believes in this principle. At the time this book is being written, we're in the midst of a building program—on a literal mountain of solid rock. It has been a 15-year journey, and we're just now beginning the first part of a six-building campus. We have spent over $7 million just to get permission to build! Our 25-acre parking lot has cost us another $9 million. It has been difficult. But we are covenant partners with Almighty God. Our congregation takes God's admonition to Zerubbabel seriously. As we drive our cars past the future site of our new campus, we roll down the windows and shout, "Grace to the mountain!" so that our difficult mountain (literally) will become a plain upon which we can build. This is a reminder to us (and to the enemy) that God is our covenant partner and that He will release His power in our behalf.

What mountains are you facing in your life? God is willing to unleash His power in your behalf (that's grace) to bring them down. This is the exchange of strengths.

exchange of weapons

The third step in the covenant-making ceremony is the ex-

We took on Jesus' enemy—

Satan. He took on our

enemy—death.

change of weapons. When Jesus and I entered into covenant, we exchanged weapons. This represents the exchange of enemies. I took on Jesus' enemy—Satan. He took on my enemy—death.

Death is the number-one enemy of humanity. We know that we cannot compete with death. It is coming to each one of us. But Jesus defeated our enemy. And because of what Jesus did, we can say, "O death, where is thy sting? O grave, where is thy victory?" (1 Cor. 15:55, KJV).

In Gen. 3:15 God speaks to Lucifer, saying, "There is enmity (strife) between you and Me" (author's paraphrase). Satan is God's enemy. Let's see how God has provided for the exchange of weapons so we can overcome His enemy. Paul writes in Eph. 6:10, "Be strong in the Lord and in the strength of *His* might" (emphasis added). Here is the exchange of strength. The covenant language continues in verse 11: "Put on the full armor of God [*His* armor], so that you will be able to stand firm against the schemes of the devil." Apparently *we* are the ones who are supposed to take on the devil. "For our struggle is not against flesh and blood" (v. 12). Not the people who irritate us or bug us. Not the spouses who may have walked away. Not the kids who may have been rebellious. Not the bosses who may have fired us. Our struggles, Paul continues, are "against the rulers, against the powers, against the world forces of this darkness, against the spiritual forces of wickedness in the heavenly places. Therefore, take up the full armor of God [note: *His* armor, thus an exchange], so that you will be able to resist in the evil day, and having done everything, to stand firm. Stand firm therefore, HAVING GIRDED YOUR LOINS WITH TRUTH, and HAVING PUT ON THE BREASTPLATE OF RIGHTEOUSNESS, and having shod YOUR FEET WITH THE PREPARATION OF THE GOSPEL OF PEACE; in addition to all, taking up the shield of faith with which you will be able to extinguish all the flaming arrows of the evil one" (vv. 12-16). This is the exchange of weapons, symbolizing the exchange of enemies. – Devil   death →Jesus

Fight with
Christ's armor

sacrifice

In the fourth step of the covenant-making ceremony, the heifer is cut on the underside and opened. In a blood covenant there is always the sacrifice of life and the shedding of blood.

In chapter 2 we talked about the heifer. In the new covenant it isn't a heifer that sheds its blood. Heb. 10:19-20 says, "We have confidence to enter the holy place by the blood of Jesus, by a new and living way which He inaugurated for us through the veil." Jesus, by choice, became the one who was slain in our covenant-making ceremony.[1]

Let's consider the historical Crucifixion event. Matt. 27:50-51 depicts Jesus hanging on the Cross just prior to dying: "Jesus cried out again with a loud voice, and yielded up His spirit. And behold, the veil of the temple was torn in two from top to bottom." The veil divided what was called the holy place from the holy of holies. History suggests that the curtain—the veil—was very thick. When Jesus died, the veil split[2] from top to bottom, recalling the imagery of slicing the heifer. The ripping also symbolizes the breaking of Jesus' flesh. It meant that believers were no longer separated from the holy of holies. There was no longer any need for a priest to mediate—the ultimate Mediator had come. Because the veil was ripped, we now have direct access to God. Jesus himself became the sacrifice—the pure, spotless Lamb of God.

walk of death   Deny self

The fifth step in the covenant-making ceremony is the walk of death. Its purpose, as one literally walked through the animal blood, was to symbolize the loss of individual identity—effectively surrendering one's life. In the New Testament Jesus says it this way: "You try to hang onto your life—you will lose it. You lay your life down for Me—you will gain it. If you pick up your cross, you will follow Me and you will die with Me." Baptism reflects the same truth. When we go down into the water, we identify with His death. When we come out of the water, we identify with His resurrection to new life—His life.

mark on the body

Step six is the covenant mark. In the old covenant a mark was placed on the body—circumcision. In the New Testament we regard circumcision a matter of the *heart*. Rom. 2:28-29 tells us, "He is not a Jew who is one outwardly, nor is circumcision that which is outward in the flesh. But he is a Jew who is one inwardly; and circumcision is that which is of the heart, by the Spirit, not by the letter; and his praise is not from men, but from God." Paul says a person is not a Jew just by virtue of having the mark of circumcision on his body; the real Jew is one who is circumcised *inwardly.* He has made a conscious, deliberate choice that he will not walk in the pathways of sinfulness any longer. Instead, he will embrace righteousness.

review and reflect

1. Why is the new covenant better than the old covenant?

2. List some examples of covenant language from the Bible.

3. What is the definition of grace in chapter 4? How is God using grace in your life right now?

4. What is the enemy of Jesus? What is the enemy of humanity? How is the enemy manifesting himself in your life situation?

5. What does "circumcision of the heart" mean?

5

the even-more-powerful new COVENANT—

continued

∞

As we continue with the steps in the covenant-making ceremony in light of the new covenant, we encounter some of the most powerful truths of the New Testament.

pronouncement of blessings and curses

The seventh step in the covenant ceremony is the pronouncement of blessings and curses. Deut. 28 says that you will be blessed if you keep the (old) covenant and cursed if you violate it. In the New Testament the blessings are found in Phil. 4:19—"My God will supply all your needs according to His riches in glory in Christ Jesus." The blessings are reiterated in Rom. 8:17—"[You are] heirs of God." What an amazing truth—*We are beneficiaries of everything He has!* In terms of the blessings of God, the resources of heaven have been released through Jesus to you because you are a joint heir with Him.

And the curses? In the New Testament we don't find the pronouncements of curses. This is the only step of the covenant ceremony that is not paralleled in the New Testament. Why?

For years I struggled to understand why the curses were missing. An experience in 1993 helped me make sense of my questions. When I lived in Dallas, I joined other Christians on Saturday mornings at abortion clinics to pray for and offer help to young women considering that option in hopes that they would choose against it. Many Christians attended, some with the organization Operation Rescue. These people often laid their bodies down in front of the door and blocked the entrance. Sometimes they were arrested for their passive protests.

As I observed the Operation Rescue volunteers, I discovered they were not a bunch of crazy fanatics, the way the media often portrayed them. They were just grandmas and grandpas, moms and dads, and teenagers. They were just normal church people who were so grieved by the thought of abortion that they literally laid their bodies in front of the clinic doors in hopes of saving lives. Every Saturday they would save at least one or two babies by their actions.

As I watched the Dallas police arrest Operation Rescue volunteers week after week, I became concerned about the officers' use of force. I contacted City Hall and raised my concerns to the office of the mayor of Dallas. As a result, Operation Rescue leaders asked me to act as a liaison between Operation Rescue and the Dallas police at these events.

In my role, I was to meet with the captain of the tactical unit and some of his key officers about three days before each rescue event took place. At one particular meeting, I was trying to persuade the police department to stop using a pressure point hold in which an officer would jam his thumb into the protestor's throat. The hold inflicted great pain, which forced an uncooperative person to walk. "You don't need to use this hold on these people," I said. "They are completely passive."

My objections seemed to fall on deaf ears, and the tactics continued. Meeting after meeting I objected.

Finally in one meeting, Dan, the tall, single, quiet leader of Operation Rescue, who was being arrested every Saturday, interrupted my dialogue with the policemen.

"Let me tell you something," he said quietly. "You don't understand. We are *not* protestors. You may know how to handle union protestors, or Ku Klux Klan protestors, or gay rights protestors. But we are *not* protestors. What we are doing is an act of repentance." Dan looked at the police officers. "We are not blaming the abortionists. We are not blaming you police officers. We are not blaming the politicians who gave us these laws. We are not blaming the young women who are pregnant, nor their partners.

"We think the blame is on *us*—the Church of Jesus Christ who have been completely silent. *We* are the problem. You people are not supposed to stand for righteousness, but the Church of Jesus Christ is. This is an *act of repentance* for our sin of silence.

"You can use the pressure point on me," Dan said. "You can do whatever you want. I don't care if you tear me limb from limb. I'm not looking for protection.

"I don't care if this Saturday you kill me. *Somewhere, somebody has to take the sin, the sickness, and the anger of this world and not pass it on.*"

When Dan said this to the policemen, I suddenly made the connection. I thought about an illustration I had heard in which upper management took their frustration out on middle management, who took it out on lower management. Then Dad went home and yelled at Mom, who scolded Junior. Junior hit his little sister, who kicked the dog, who bit the cat. The cycle never stopped. The anger simply continued being passed on.

Jesus became the "Grand Shock Absorber," taking on the curses, fury, sickness, and sins of the ages. He absorbed the sin and the pain, and He didn't pass it on.

Dan said it again. *"Someone has to absorb the sin and the pain and not pass it on.* We'll take full responsibility for the sin of abortion in this nation."

With those words, I suddenly understood what had puzzled me for more than a decade. I now knew why there was no pronouncement of curses in the New Testament. You see, Jesus became the "Grand Shock Absorber," taking on the curses, fury, sickness, and sins of the ages. He absorbed the sin and the pain, and He didn't pass it on. That's why Gal. 3:13 says, "CURSED IS EVERYONE WHO HANGS ON A TREE." In other words, Jesus "filters out" the horrible curses so that the blessings can come through. The next verse states "that in Christ Jesus the blessing of Abraham might come" (v. 14). So instead of "cursed are you," the New Testament knows only "blessed are you." The pronouncement of blessings and curses becomes, in the New Testament, the *absorption of curses* by Jesus and the *pronouncement of blessings* on all of us. We are free from the curse of sin!

One of the most moving examples of Jesus' taking of the curse is found in the very first scripture we examined regarding the covenant, Gen. 15 (see chapter 2). In that passage, God made a covenant with Abram. True to covenant tradition, a heifer was cut in two. Then the two individuals who made the covenant were supposed to walk between the two halves. But Abram didn't do this. In fact, he slept through the whole event (v. 12). It would be as if a groom fell asleep before his wedding and missed the ceremony. How could this happen?

The answer to this question is simple. *God* caused him to fall asleep. But why? Because anyone making covenant (walking between the halves of a heifer) must be able to keep the covenant *perfectly.* And God knew Abram could not do that. So what did He do? He arranged for someone else to walk between the halves. In fact, God did it himself.[1] Gen. 15:17 states that a smoking oven and a flaming torch passed between the halves of the heifer. What is a smoking oven? Whenever God the Father showed up in the Old Testament, He frequently came in the form of fire. And that's what He did in Gen. 15. But what's the second form, the flaming torch? According to some writers, this was the second member of the Trinity, Jesus himself.[2] Gen. 15 isn't the only passage that uses the word "flaming" or "flame" to describe Him. On three occasions in Revelation (1:14; 2:18; 19:12) John uses the term to depict Jesus.

But why would Jesus walk through the halves of the heifer? Because He represented Abram. Jesus represented Abram (and his spiritual descendants), and because they did *not* keep the covenant perfectly, it cost Him His life. Even here, back in Gen. 15:17, Jesus was taking the curse of humanity.

Abraham couldn't or wouldn't

covenant meal

The eighth step is the covenant meal. "I am the bread of life," Jesus says in John 6:48. In this passage Jesus is in a discussion with the Pharisees, and, as usual, they are spiritually dull—they just don't get it. "Your fathers ate the manna in the wilderness, and they died," Jesus says. "This is the bread which comes down out of heaven, so that one may eat of it and not die. I am the living bread that came down out of heaven; if anyone eats of this bread, he will live forever; and the bread also which I will give for the life of the world is My flesh" (vv. 49-51).

Verse 52 tells us how the Pharisees responded: "The Jews began to argue with one another, saying, 'How can this man give us His flesh to eat?'" The Pharisees are wondering if Jesus is encouraging them to cannibalism! In reality, He is saying to them, "*I* am your covenant meal. *I* am living bread for you. If you take of *Me*, if you absorb *Me*, you will have life. Without

Me, it's over for you. Without Me, you're dead. But with Me, you live—*really* live!"

This truth is reiterated in 1 Cor. 11—"When He had given thanks, He broke it [the bread] and said, 'This is My body, which is for you; do this in remembrance of Me.' In the same way He took the cup also after supper, saying, 'This cup is the new covenant in My blood; do this, as often as you drink it, in remembrance of Me.' For as often as you eat this bread and drink the cup, you proclaim the Lord's death until He comes. Therefore whoever eats the bread or drinks the cup of the Lord in an unworthy manner, shall be guilty of the body and the blood of the Lord. But a man must examine himself. . . . For he who eats and drinks, eats and drinks judgment to himself if he does not judge the body rightly" (vv. 24-29). Before we participate in the covenant meal (the Lord's Supper or Communion), we must examine ourselves. We should not participate in covenant or the covenant meal flippantly. Entering into covenant is a serious thing. In fact, verse 30 states that by *not* taking the covenant seriously, some had died. It is not to be taken lightly.

exchange of names

The ninth step in the covenant is the exchange of names. How is that paralleled in the New Testament? We take upon ourselves His name, Christ. Christ-*ian*. The *ian* denotes one who is of somebody else. I became a Christ-*ian:* one who is of Christ. And He took upon himself *my* name. How did He do that? He could have rightly called himself the Son of God, but He chose to call himself repeatedly "the Son of Man."

Ps 20:7

exchange of the oldest male child – See p 40

In an earlier chapter it was stated that the tenth step in the

In Abraham's heart Isaac

had already been dead,

figuratively speaking,

for three days. God

"resurrected him,"

again figuratively,

on the third day.

covenant-making ceremony is very important, although no details were provided. Let's examine it.

The final step is the exchange of the oldest male child. Tradition stated that in order to "seal" the agreement, to *prove* the covenant was for real, the partners would exchange oldest sons. The sons would actually move into the home of the partner to be raised. It was a painful event, but one that would prove the covenant was for real.

In the most painful test of his lifetime, Abram lived out this last step of the covenant partnership. Gen. 22:1-2 tells us, "God *tested* Abraham, and said to him, 'Abraham!' And he said, 'Here I am.' He said, 'Take now your son.'" Abraham didn't balk; He knew that exchanging sons was part of the covenant-making ceremony. If he was going to receive what God promised him, he had to give his son to God. So Isaac headed up the mountain with Abraham. Some suggest that he was around 33 years of age,[3] though that is impossible to verify.

Eventually the young man asked his father where they would get the animal they were to sacrifice. "Yahweh Jireh" Abraham answered. "God will provide."

The moment of truth arrived; Abraham raised the knife. Heb. 11:17 tells us that in his heart Abraham had already sacrificed Isaac. Gen. 22:4 notes that "on the third day Abraham raised his eyes and saw the place from a distance." In other words, in Abraham's heart Isaac had already been dead, figuratively speaking, for three days. God "resurrected him," again figuratively, on the third day. "By faith Abraham, when he was tested, offered up Isaac, and he who had received the promises was offering up his only begotten son" (Heb. 11:17). How could he do this?

Scripture gives us a glimpse into Abraham's thinking. Isaac was his only son. Yet Abraham knew that God had promised

And just like Isaac, who

was "dead" for three days

in Abraham's heart,

Jesus, too,

was in the tomb for

three days—and then

came the Resurrection.

him that his descendants would come through the line of Isaac and outnumber the stars in heaven. Heb. 11:19 continues: "He considered that God is able to raise people even from the dead." Abraham's confidence in the covenant-keeping God was so great that he believed God would give Isaac back to him through resurrection. In effect God, when He stopped Abraham from sacrificing Isaac, was saying, "Abraham, I've seen your heart. It's as if you've already sacrificed him. You know that I would have to resurrect him since he's the 'promise child.' And your confidence in Me is so great, you really believe I'll do exactly that, so let's save both of us some time. You don't need to go any further in this ceremony. Stop now. Lay down the knife. You've already passed the test."

Gen. 22:16-17 says, "By Myself I have sworn, declares the LORD, *because you* have *done this thing* [What thing? Sacrificed Isaac] *and have not withheld your son,* your only son, indeed I will greatly bless you" (emphasis added). God goes on to promise Abraham many offspring: "Your seed shall possess the gate of their enemies. In your seed all the nations of the earth shall be blessed" (vv. 17-18). Ultimately this exchange of the oldest male child would be paralleled in the sacrifice of Jesus, which inaugurated the new covenant. "Abraham, because you gave up your only child, now I will give up *My* only child," God in effect said. This is the powerful, revolutionary truth of the covenant. Isaac likely carried the wood for the sacrifice of his own body up the hill named Mount Moriah. Likewise, Jesus carried the wood (a cross) for the sacrifice of His own body up the same hill, or a hill nearby.

And just like Isaac, who was "dead" for three days in Abraham's heart[4] (Gen. 22:4), Jesus, too, was in the tomb for three days—and then came the Resurrection. "The covenant has been tested," God in essence said. "It will stand. Now the covenant is firm."

God continued to elaborate on Abraham's obedience. "Your descendants are going to possess the gates of your enemies," He said.

possessing the gates

What is the significance of possessing the gates? Gates are where a city is controlled. In Bible times the elders of the city would sit by the gates, determining who entered and who left. They controlled all commerce; they controlled all political life. Essentially, the gatekeepers controlled the city. God promises Abraham that his descendants would be the gatekeepers—possess the gates—even of their enemies.

In the 16th chapter of Matthew we read, "When Jesus came into the district of Caesarea Philippi, He was asking His disciples, 'Who do people say that the Son of Man is?' [In more contemporary language, "What's being reported in the *Jerusalem Times*? Who do they say I am in the *Jordan Post*?"] And they said, 'Some say John the Baptist' [because You baptize]; and others, Elijah [because You perform miracles]; but still others, Jeremiah [because You weep over the city], or one of the prophets." Jesus persisted: "'But who do you say that I am?' Simon Peter answered, 'You are the Christ, the Son of the living God.'" It became very quiet. No one had ever stated this before! Peter was always the first to speak. And tragically, he often said something stupid. But not this time. Peter was right on.

"And Jesus said to him, 'Blessed are you, Simon Barjona [Simon's other name was "Rock." "Bar" means "son of." "Jona" means "John." What Jesus was saying here is "You're great, Rocky Johnson!"], because flesh and blood did not reveal this to you, but My

Father who is in heaven. [In other words, "You didn't learn this in seminary, from a book, or in listening to a tape. My Father showed you this—directly!"] I also say to you that you are Peter, and upon this rock [*petra* in the Greek; upon the rock of this revelation—what revelation? That You, Jesus, are the Son of the living God. Upon the rock of who Jesus is] I will build My church; and the *gates* of Hades will not overpower it'" (vv. 13-18, emphasis added). In fact, you will go in and rip the gates right off the hinges. In other words, the Church has authority—covenant authority.

Jesus continues in verse 19: "I will give you the keys of the kingdom of heaven; and whatever you bind on earth shall have been bound in heaven, and whatever you loose on earth shall have been loosed in heaven."

When God says that on the rock of this revelation (the reality of who Jesus Christ is) He is going to build His Church and that you are going to rip the gates of hell right off the hinges, what does He mean? He means that we have the keys, that we control not only our city but the enemies' city as well. We can put a stop to what the enemy is doing. When we pray, speak, or declare God's will (not our own), God supports us, because it's *His* authority we're exercising. Prayer is powerful when we've aligned ourselves with *His* exciting will, *His* "game plan." Listen to the powerful truth expressed in the *Amplified Bible:* "I will give you the keys to the kingdom of heaven; and whatever you bind (declare to be improper and unlawful) on earth must be what is already bound in heaven; and whatever you loose (declare lawful) on earth must be what is already loosed in heaven" (v. 19, AMP.).

It's that principle of authority again. If I have the keys to my car, I'm the one who can drive my car. If I give the keys to you, now you can drive my car. Why? Because you have the *keys.* The person who has the keys has the authority.

parity treaty vs. suzerain treaty

In biblical times there were two kinds of treaties: a parity treaty and suzerain treaty.[5] If you and a friend enter into a covenant, it is called a parity treaty, because you are nearly equal. But if a king, who owns everything, enters into a treaty with a peasant, who has nothing, it is called a suzerain treaty. In this case, when the two parties come together to exchange all their assets and strengths, the conversation might go something like this:

"I don't have anything," the peasant says.

"I know—I have everything, and you have nothing," the king answers.

"What am I going to give you, then?"

"The one thing you have," the king says.

"What's that?"

"You! Your love, your loyalty, and your commitment. That's all you have to give. That's what I want."

what God is asking from us

The covenant between God and us is *not* a parity covenant[6] —it is a suzerain covenant, between a King who has everything and us, who have nothing.

"I'm going to give you everything I have," God says. "It's yours: heaven's resources at your disposal right now."

"I don't have anything to give, God," we respond.

"I know. I've always known."

"All I have is me."

"That's what I want," God affirms.

"All I have is my love and my loyalty," we insist.

"That's exactly what I'm asking for."

And that's what He's asking from me—and from you.

Prayer: *O God, help us to understand how to walk in covenant. In Jesus' name. Amen.*

review and reflect

1. List the blessings of the covenant. How have you seen these demonstrated in your life?

2. List the Old Testament curses from the covenant ceremony. Why aren't these repeated in the New Testament?

3. Discuss the significance of the covenant meal.

4. Abraham faced the biggest test of his lifetime when God called him to sacrifice Isaac. What has been the biggest test of your lifetime?

5. How could God help you possess the gates of your enemy?

6. What are the implications of holding the "keys" to the Kingdom?

Read. 6+7

6

the planting of a tree—
a reminder of the
COVENANT

∞

In previous chapters we covered the 10 steps of the covenant-making ceremony. An analysis of the ceremony in primitive cultures reveals that memorials, or reminders, were designed to prevent either party from forgetting the covenant. We'll mention two of them in this and the next chapter. Let's look at the first one—the planting of a tree.

the place of the oath

In Gen. 21:31-33 we read these words: "Therefore he called that place Beersheba, because there the two of them took an oath. So they made a covenant at Beersheba; and Abimelech and Phicol, the commander of his army, arose and returned to the land of the Philistines. Abraham planted a tamarisk tree at Beersheba, and there he called on the name of the LORD, the Everlasting God." This is an example of another step of the covenant-making ceremony, the planting of a tree. In this case it was a tamarisk tree, which is considered to be part of the palm family. In the Old Testament the palm is seen as the symbol of victory. Abraham and the Philistines entered into a covenant through the planting of the tree.

Personally, I find this step a rather intriguing one. For many years I have given trees as gifts to very special friends. In elementary school my fifth grade teacher, Ethel Henthorne, gave me a crabapple tree. I planted it, and it grew from a tiny sapling to a very large tree. Every time I looked at it, I thought of that outstanding teacher. I was so excited about that type of gift that through the years I have given trees and planted them for special friends, all the while not realizing that this was God's pattern for reminding people of their commitments.

the trees of the garden

In the very beginning of the Bible we see the importance that God placed upon a tree. In Gen. 2 we read that God placed Adam and Eve in that phenomenal location known as the Garden of Eden. He allowed them to eat from any tree, with the single exception of the tree of the knowledge of good and evil. Numerous interpretations have been given for this particular tree. I believe it represented God's presence. It was reserved for God alone, for it is God who determines what is good and what is evil. The individual's attempt to eat from that tree indicates a desire to preempt God and to determine what is good and what is evil. In our worst moments, we continually try to "play God" and determine our own set of right and wrong. If we picture good on the right-hand side and evil on the left-hand side, with a demarcation between them, we see that humanity continually tries to move the line to the left—in other words, declaring things that God has called evil to actually be good. That's what happens in Isa. 5:20, which states that humanity has a tendency to call good things bad and bad things good. Simply stated, this is humanity eating of the tree of the knowledge of good and evil.

As a consequence, Adam and Eve were ordered out of the garden: "Then the LORD God said, 'Behold, the man has become like one of Us, knowing good and evil; and now, he might stretch out his hand, and take also from the tree of life, and eat, and live forever'—therefore the LORD God sent him out from the garden of Eden, to cultivate the ground from which he was taken. So He drove the man out; and at the east of the garden of Eden He stationed the cherubim and the flaming sword which turned every direction to guard the way to the tree of life" (Gen. 3:22-24).

Now humanity, having chosen sin and having violated the covenant of the Garden of Eden, was taken away from the tree of life—the tree they most needed. Whenever people "eat of the tree of the knowledge of good and evil," that is, make themselves to be their own god, they lose access to the tree of life, that is, they bring death upon themselves. But that's not the end of the story. We've been looking at the very first few pages of the Bible. Let's go all the way to the last page to follow the story in this climax.

In Rev. 22:8-9, 14, 17, John writes, "I, John, am the one who heard and saw these things. And when I heard and saw, I fell down to worship at the feet of the angel who showed me these things. But he said to me, 'Do not do that. I am a fellow servant of yours' . . . Blessed are those who wash their robes, so that they may have *the right to the tree of life,* and may enter by the gates into the city. . . . The Spirit and the bride say, *'Come.'* And let the one who hears say, *'Come.'* And let the one who is thirsty come; let the one who wishes take the water of life without cost" (emphasis added).

the impact of calvary's tree

Notice the radical change from Genesis. In Genesis a guard was put around the tree of life. Adam and Eve were cast out; they had no access to the tree that would provide life for them. But in the closing verses of the last chapter of the entire Bible the tone is precisely the opposite. The angel of the Lord says, "Don't be afraid—you're welcome here." And as if that's not enough, we're informed that we have a *right* to come to the tree of life and we can enter through the gates of the city to get to it. We don't have to climb over any walls. And then as if even that's not enough, there's even more. The Spirit says, "Come." And He even says it a second time: "Come." We are *invited* to the tree of life.

What's the difference? What happened between the first few pages of Genesis and the final few pages of Revelation? Well, you guessed it. There are two more trees. In the story in which Isaac perhaps carried the wood for the sacrifice up the hill, the Hebrew word for "wood" and "tree" are the same. When the Abrahamic covenant was sealed and confirmed that day, God was essentially saying to Abraham, "Since you have honored this covenant by giving your only son, I can honor this covenant by giving *My* only Son." And Jesus was crucified on a cross, or "tree"—Calvary's "tree"—which made possible the access for all of us back to the Tree of Life, Jesus himself. It's Calvary's tree that caused the tone of the "Get out" in Gen. 3 to be changed to "Come in" in Rev. 22. The planting of a tree is a significant part in the covenant-making ceremony.

ancient tribes

Even in primitive tribes of the East, this tree-planting practice was followed. In Burma this has been followed through the centuries. In Timor, Trumbull reports that a fig tree was a witness to the rite of covenant-making. It is stated that one missionary had to "cut covenant" over 50 times with different tribes in order to have an effective and safe stay. When he entered into the tree-planting aspect of the covenant, a chieftain informed the people of his tribe that Mr. Stanley was now their "beloved brother."[1] It is believed that the reason the trees at Hebron are so prominent in Scripture is that they were actually witnesses to the covenant being made between Abraham and three Amorite chiefs (Gen. 13:18; 14:13; 18:1).

the blood-stained tree

Not only is it intriguing that primitive cultures establish covenant by tree planting, but it is even more fascinating that some cultures have practiced this rite by a blood-stained "fiery cross" as a part of their tree-planting covenant-making ceremony. This occurred both in the Scottish Highlands in primitive culture, as well as in the southeastern portion of Arabia. It's significant that the tree was soaked with the blood from the throat of a sheep. The bloody branch was then placed into the earth.[2] The potential symbolism of this ancient rite is profound in its comparison to the blood-drenched tree of Calvary that was stained by the blood of the Lamb of God.

review and reflect

1. Why would the planting of a tree be part of a covenant?

2. What did the first covenant tree represent?

3. Why did God refuse to allow Adam and Eve to eat of the tree?

4. At the end of the Bible another tree is mentioned. Why are we invited to this tree?

7

stones and mountains
—more reminders of the
COVENANT

∞

We are now continuing our examination of the memorials that were designed to remind people of the covenant that had been made. One such reminder is the use of stones. This practice is found in sources outside biblical times. As an example, Arabians would initiate a covenant by making an incision on the hand or the wrist and then allowing the blood to drip onto seven stones. These stones were then a permanent reminder that they had made covenant.[1]

the stone at bethel

However, our concern here is not with nonbiblical sources, but with biblical examples of the covenant. One of the earliest references to stones being used as covenant reminders is found in Gen. 28:18-22, which states: "So Jacob rose early in the morning, and took the stone that he had put under his head and set it up as a pillar and poured oil on its top. He called the name of that place Bethel; however, previously the name of the city had been Luz. Then Jacob made a vow, saying, 'If God will be with me and will keep me on this journey that I take, and will give me food to eat and garments to wear, and I return to my father's house in safety, then the LORD will be my God. This stone, which I have set up as a pillar, will be God's house, and of all that You give me I will surely give a tenth to You.'" One of the reasons stones are popular as a covenant reminder is their permanence. They could be counted on to be in place for several generations.

the witness stone

Another example of stones being used as a covenant reminder is found in Gen. 31:45-53. "Then Jacob took a stone and set it up as a pillar. Jacob said to his kinsmen, 'Gather stones.' So they took stones and made a heap, and they ate there by the heap. Now Laban called it Jegar-sahadutha ["the heap of witness" in Aramaic—in other words, a reminder or witness to their covenant], but Jacob called it Galeed [which also means "the heap of witness" but in Hebrew]. Laban said, 'This heap is a witness between you and me this day.' Therefore it was named Galeed" (vv. 45-48).

In the next few verses Jacob and Laban admonish each other that this pile of stones is a continual reminder of how they are to treat each other. In true covenant fashion they announce both blessings and curses, stating that neither one is ever to walk by this with intent of doing harm to the other. And they both remind each other that God is a witness and that He will see this. In verse 49 they even refer to this as Mizpah, which means a watchtower, signifying that God is watching over them. The point is that this pile of stones was to be a visual aid to recalling the implications of covenant making and covenant keeping.

the intergenerational reminder

One of the most exhilarating passages on stones being used as a covenant reminder is Josh. 4. The fascinating part of this passage is that the stones were to be a reminder to the next generation. Remember that covenant is always *multi*generational. The Lord instructed Joshua to pile up 12 stones as a reminder of God's faithfulness as they crossed the Jordan River into the Promised Land. They had waited so long for this moment, but God slowed them down just long enough to leave a permanent mark for the sake of future generations.

"This pile of stones will be a reminder for you," Joshua said to the people, "When our children ask in later years, 'What are these stones here for? Why are they piled up like this?' then we will have an answer for them" (Josh. 4:6-7, author's paraphrase). In verses 21-24 of the same chapter, after they had put the stones in place, Joshua reminded them again, "When your children ask their fathers in time to come, saying, 'What are these stones?' then you shall inform your children, saying, 'Israel crossed this Jordan on dry ground.' For the LORD your God dried up the waters of the Jordan before you until you had crossed, just as the LORD your God had done to the Red Sea, which He dried up before us until we had crossed; that all the peoples of the earth may know that the hand of the LORD is mighty, so that you may fear the LORD your God forever."

What a thrill it must have been when many of the younger ones who had crossed the Jordan came back in their later years with their children and grandchildren and heard their grandchildren ask, "Grandpa, why are these stones here?" With a smile, they would tell the story of God's faithfulness many years before. This was a reminder of a covenant that God had not only made but also kept. And He kept it for the future generations as well.

the "stone of help"

In 1 Sam. 7:5-12 the Israelites used a stone as a reminder of God's covenant love for them. The Philistines were about to attack the Israelites, but God caused a great thunder to confuse them. The result was a resounding victory for Israel once again. Samuel then took a large stone and placed it between Mizpah and Shen, and he named it Ebenezer, which translates "the stone of help." This stone was not so much a reminder of a covenant made but a covenant kept—on the part of God. He had once again protected them as He had promised.

the stone of warning

If a stone is a reminder of the covenant blessings, it can also be a reminder of the curses that can befall one who does not maintain the covenant. In Josh. 24:26-27 we read that Joshua placed a large stone under an oak tree and informed the people, "This stone shall be for a witness against us, for it has heard all the words of the LORD which He spoke to us; thus it shall be for a witness against you, so that you do not deny your God" (v. 27).

god as stone

Ironically, God himself is referred to as "the Stone of Israel" in Gen. 49:24. And again, in Dan. 2:34-35, He is portrayed as a stone that strikes and crushes all others and literally becomes a great mountain that fills the entire earth. This profound reference to Jesus is repeated again in the New Testament in Matt. 21:44, in which anyone who falls on the stone is broken, or if the stone falls on the person, it simply scatters him or her.

Both the Old and the New Testaments portray Jesus as the stone, but this time as a cornerstone. In Ps. 118:22 and in Matt. 21:42, Jesus is depicted as the cornerstone, the main stone of the building. He was placed there by the Father after the builders (i.e., the Pharisees) rejected Him.

Paul takes the analogy considerably further in Eph. 2:19-22 when he speaks of God's household. The foundation is what has been preached by the apostles and the prophets. Jesus Christ is the cornerstone of this building, by which the entire building is "fitted together," or held intact. It is Jesus, according to verse 22, who brings us together, thus making us "a dwelling of God."

mountains as covenant reminders

To this point we've looked only at stones. Let's take a moment to look at the role mountains play in reminding people of the covenant. In Deut. 11:26-29, Moses preached the second of his three sermons that fill the Book of Deuteronomy. He described one of the steps of the covenant once again: the pronouncement of blessings and curses. The Hebrews were reminded that if they obeyed the Lord, they would experience blessings. If they violated God's ways, they would bring the curse upon themselves. He told the children of Israel that when they finally entered the Promised Land after waiting so long, he wanted them to have an additional reminder of the blessings and curses so they would choose to walk in obedience and experience the blessings. He identified Mount Gerizim with blessings and Mount Ebal with curses.

He repeated this in his third and final sermon, found in Deut. 27:12-13: "When you cross the Jordan, these shall stand on Mount Gerizim to bless the people [and he lists their names] . . . For the curse, these shall stand on Mount Ebal [and then he lists the names of those who are to be on that mountain]."

The children of Israel were finally crossing the Jordan. As they did, God took them through one more step of the covenant-making ceremony, the pronouncement of blessings and curses. He wanted some visual aids, specifically mountains, to be reminders to them of the covenant He had with them. A group of people stood on Mount Gerizim and spoke blessings on the people: "Blessed shall you be if you obey the Lord your God." At the same time a group of people stood on Mount Ebal and reminded the people of the consequences for disobedience: "Cursed shall you be if you violate the way of the Lord."

the walk between the mountains

But Moses never actually got to see this happen. He only *asked* them to do it on two different occasions in two different sermons. It was up to Joshua to live out this unusual exercise in the covenant-making ceremony, and he did precisely that. Josh. 8:33-34 states, "All Israel with their elders and officers and their judges were standing on both sides of the ark before the Levitical priests who carried the ark of the covenant of the LORD, the stranger as well as the native. Half of them stood in front of Mount Gerizim and half of them in front of Mount Ebal, just as Moses the servant of the LORD had given command at first to bless the people of Israel. Then afterward he read all the words of the law, the blessing and the curse, according to all that is written in the book of the law."

Precisely how this occurred is not told in the text. Here is the mental picture I have of it, although I admit I may have taken poetic license at this point. As the children of Israel passed into Israel, a group of people shouted down from Mount Gerizim, "Blessed shall you be if you obey the Lord your God!" The children of Israel looked to the south, to their left, to see people yelling down from Mount Gerizim, speaking the blessing. But as soon as they heard those wonderful words, they heard something much less enjoyable. From Mount Ebal, to the north, would come this stark challenge: "Cursed shall you be if you disobey the Lord your God. Cursed shall be you and your children and your cattle and your oxen and your donkeys. Cursed shall you be in everything you set out to do." The startled children of Israel would gaze to their right, up to Mount Ebal, and see the people who were yelling this grave warning.

the power of a reminder

A few months later the Israelites were well settled in the Promised Land. On one particular day one of the young men contemplated involving himself in a wicked act. He thought about it for a moment and realized nobody would see him, so he went to the place where he was ready to execute his act of wickedness. Just before his participation in sin, he glanced around one final time to see if anybody was watching. His eyes were arrested—not by another person, however, but by two mountains in the distance. One was Mount Gerizim, the other Mount Ebal. He paused for a moment. He looked at the mountains a little longer, and then he recalled that day, the day they had crossed the Jordan. He remembered that from Mount Gerizim they had been reminded that obedience always resulted in blessing. He felt a chill on his spine when he remembered what was said from the other mountain, however. From Mount Ebal the people had shouted that if you violated the ways of God, curses would come upon you. He paused a moment longer, realizing he did not want a curse to be upon him. He desired blessings. Under great conviction, he turned from the sin he was about to commit and made his way back home. That's the way I picture it. Thus was the important role of mountains in the making and keeping of a covenant.

mount sinai vs. mount zion

No more poignant description of the differences between two mountains occurs anywhere in the scripture than what is found in Heb. 12. Two mountains are contrasted: one is a place of fear; the other is a place of hope: "You have not come to a mountain that can be touched and to a blazing fire, and to darkness and gloom and whirlwind, and to the blast of a trumpet and the sound of words which sound was such that those who heard begged that no further word be spoken to them. For they could not bear the command, 'IF EVEN A BEAST TOUCHES THE MOUNTAIN, IT WILL BE STONED.' And so terrible was the sight, that Moses said, 'I AM FULL OF FEAR and trembling.' But you have come to Mount Zion . . . and to Jesus, the mediator of a new covenant, and to the sprinkled blood, which speaks better than the blood of Abel" (Heb. 12:18-22, 24).

Look at the indescribable difference in these mountains. One is a place of terror (v. 18). It is Mount Sinai, where the Law was given. The Law said that if you did not keep it perfectly, you would suffer the full consequences of your failure. Everyone knew he or she couldn't keep the Law perfectly. Consequently, Mount Sinai was a place of law, judgment, and destruction.

But you haven't come to that mountain, the writer of Hebrews says. You have come to a completely different one. You have come to Mount Zion (which generally refers to the Church), and to the place where righteous persons were made perfect. How were these men made perfect? They were made perfect by Jesus, the One who mediated a new covenant. He died for all the covenant breakers so they would not have to. Consequently, they got to enjoy the benefit of a perfectly kept covenant.

The writer of Hebrews goes on to say it was Jesus' sprinkled

Though we deserve to die,

we have blessing instead.

This is the kind of

mountain (Mount Zion)

we have come to. It is the

mount of blessing.

blood that they had come to. The very sprinkling of blood is one more step in the covenant-making ceremony.

the blood "speaks"

But there's even more. The writer of Hebrews says that this blood "speaks." And what does it say? It speaks "better than the blood of Abel." Remember that Abel was the first person ever murdered. What does it mean that Abel's blood "speaks"? In the ancient world inanimate objects were frequently personified, that is, given human dimensions and personality. In this particular case, it is blood that is portrayed as talking. Jesus' blood talks—and whatever it says is "better" than what is said by the blood of Abel.[2]

That raises an obvious question: what does the blood of Abel say? For that, we go to Gen. 4:10-11: "The voice of your brother's blood is crying to Me from the ground. Now you are cursed from the ground." That is what Abel's blood said. It said that Cain, the one who murdered Abel, would die. He was cursed. But the writer of Hebrews tells us that Jesus' blood doesn't say that; rather, we are told that though we deserve to die, we have blessing instead. This is the kind of mountain (Mount Zion) we have come to. It is the mount of blessing. Mount Sinai had become the mount of curses, but Mount Zion (referring to our relationship with God through the Church) is the place of blessings. That's why the writer stressed that Jesus' blood says better things than the blood of Abel does. In other words, Jesus' blood is our place of refuge. It is the place where we find safety; it is the place of mercy.

the cities of refuge

One of the most profound depictions of Jesus in the Old

Testament is found in Num. 35:9-34. It is a description of the cities of refuge. If one inadvertently took the life of another, the passage says he was to run quickly to one of these six cities. If you made it to the city, you were free. You would not have to pay for the death you had inadvertently caused. This was the place of safety.

Jesus is our "city of refuge." He is the place we run to, and, as a result, we enjoy our safety in Him. We find mercy.

review and reflect

1. Why was the use of stones popular as covenant reminders?

2. What does it mean to "raise an Ebenezer"?

3. How might mountains have figured in the role of keeping a covenant?

4. How does Mount Sinai differ from Mount Zion in covenant metaphor? What correlation do you see between the two mountains (Zion and Sinai) in chapter 7 and the two trees in chapter 6?

8

exercising the authority of the COVENANT

∞

How do we take the covenant teaching and apply it to our lives? Understanding the covenant and living in its authority is fundamental to the victorious Christian life. Grasping the significance of the covenant is imperative if the Church is to carry on the work of Jesus.

our need for authority

The purpose of the Church is to continue what Jesus started. One problem with the Church today is that it does many things Jesus doesn't call it to do.

But if we're going to do what Jesus did, we need to understand authority. In Luke 10:19 Jesus said, "Behold, I have given you authority to tread on serpents and scorpions, and over all the power of the enemy, and nothing will injure you." Jesus said this to 70 relatively new Christians. They had been believers for less than three years, possibly less than that; yet He sent them out to change the world.

lessons from a soldier

Let's hold that story a moment and go to another passage dealing with authority. Matt. 8:5-13 tells us the story of the centurion, a military official responsible for 100 people: "And when Jesus entered Capernaum, a centurion came to Him, imploring Him, and saying, 'Lord, my servant is lying paralyzed at home, fearfully tormented.' Jesus said to him, 'I will come and heal him.' But the centurion said, 'Lord, I am not worthy for You to come under my roof, but just say the word, and my servant will be healed. For I, too, am a man under authority, with soldiers under me; and I say to this one, 'Go!' and he goes, and to another, 'Come!' and he comes, and to my slave, 'Do this!' and he does it" (vv. 5-9).

Jesus' surprise is evident: "Now when Jesus heard this, He marveled and said to those who were following, 'Truly I say to you, I have not found such great faith with anyone in Israel'" (v. 10). Then Jesus says something that seems unrelated to the situation: "I say to you, that many will come from east and west [those are the Gentiles, outside Israel, and outside the covenant at this point], and recline at the table with Abraham, Isaac and Jacob in the kingdom of heaven [that's the Abrahamic covenant and the blessings this covenant brings]. . . . And Jesus said to the centurion, 'Go; it shall be done for you as you have believed.' And the servant was healed that very moment" (vv. 11, 13).

faith and authority

There's a direct relationship between living by faith, authentic "Jesus faith," and understanding authority. The centurion understood this. "You don't need to come all the way to my house," he said. "I'm a military leader; I understand authority. I have men under me. When I say move, they move. Jesus, just speak the word, and it will happen."

"I haven't seen faith like this in all of Israel," Jesus replied. "Not even among the 'covenant children,' who are supposed to understand the covenant." There's a relationship in learning how to live by faith and understanding our authority in Christ. Let's consider those two together.

tracing authority

In the beginning, God gave authority to humanity, specifically to Adam. Gen. 1:26 says, "Let Us make man in Our image, according to Our likeness; and *let them rule* [some translations say "have dominion"] over the fish of the sea and over the birds of the sky and over the cattle and over all the earth, and over every creeping thing that creeps on the earth" (emphasis added). Having received "authority" or "dominion" means that God has given you rule over something that isn't yours. The same word is used for "steward" or "stewardship." We have responsibility over something that doesn't belong to us.

Most of us drive our own cars. But if we borrow a friend's car, we drive very carefully, because we know it's not ours. While the car is in our possession, we have the authority and the responsibility to take care of it. So it is with the earth. We "steward" it—have authority over it—but it isn't ours.

Ps. 8:4-6 confirms that we have this kind of authority: "What is man that You take thought of him, and the son of man that You care for him? Yet You have made him a little lower than God, and You crown him with glory and majesty! *You make him to rule over the works of Your hands;* You have put all things under his feet" (emphasis added). As these verses show, God gave significant authority to humanity.

adam "fumbled the ball"

However, this profound authority, given in Gen. 1:26, was lost: Adam surrendered his God-given authority to Satan. Simply put, Adam "fumbled the ball," and Satan picked it up and ran with it. Gen. 3 tells how the serpent approached Eve and planted a seed of doubt: "Did God really say . . . ?" Eve answered: "From the fruit of the tree which is in the middle of the garden, God has said, 'You shall not eat from it or touch it, or you will die.' The serpent said to the woman, 'You surely will not die!'" (vv. 3-4). Here the serpent boldly challenged God's authority; the ruse worked. "When the woman saw that the tree was good for food, and that it was a delight to the eyes, and that the tree was desirable to make one wise, she took from its fruit and ate; and she gave also to her husband with her, and he ate" (v. 6).

Where was Adam in all this? As a preacher once said, he wasn't out naming bugs and picking berries. He was in the garden too, but he failed to exercise authority over the enemy. Adam could have said, "In the name of Almighty God, who gave me dominion, authority, and rule over the earth, I command you to be gone"—and that would have been the end of it. But he *didn't* exercise his God-given authority, and because of this, we paid a terrible price for his failure.

exercising authority

If Adam really had that kind of authority, how should he have exercised it? God modeled the preferred method throughout Genesis. In 1:3, 6, 9, 11, 14, 20, 24, 26, and 29 the scriptures read, "Then God said . . ." God didn't just *think* things into existence; He *spoke* them. He looked around the universe and said, "It's dark out here—let there be light." And light was.

Words have authority

in the realm

of the Spirit.

Heb. 11:2 tells us that the worlds were framed by the *word* of God. Likewise, when Christians exercise spiritual authority, we do it by speaking.

Words have authority in the realm of the Spirit. Like seeds, they are planted, and we reap a harvest—good or bad. In Gen. 1:12 we find the "law of Genesis"—"The earth brought forth vegetation, plants yielding seed after their kind, and trees bearing fruit with seed in them, after their kind; and God saw that it was good."

I grew up on a farm. Not once did we plant wheat and then harvest corn. Not once did we plant cucumbers and then discover that we had grown strawberries. The law of Genesis is this: *Everything produces after its own kind.*

The implications are enormous—especially for people with authority. We exert our authority by speaking it. When a pastor tells the congregation to stand, the people stand. If a teacher, a coach, a boss, a parent says to do something, those under his or her direction follow (or at least are supposed to). The power of the spoken word points to part of the reason prayer is powerful and important. It helps us to see why soaking our spirits with the words God has spoken—the Bible—is essential for growth, so that we speak His way, His will, and His word. We are people who operate in the authority of the covenant—we should be cautious with what we say and mindful of the power of the spoken word.

from the physical to the spiritual

The law of sowing and reaping works just as surely in the *spiritual* domain as it does in the physical domain. Consider Luke 17:5-6, "The apostles said to the Lord, 'Increase our faith!' And the Lord said, 'If you had faith like a mustard seed, you would say to this mulberry tree, 'Be uprooted and be planted in the sea'; and it would obey you." Is Jesus trying to teach the disciples the fine art of tree uprooting? No. He's giving them a key to His kingdom. In the previous verses, 1-4, Jesus gave some very difficult instruction. Look at verses 3-4: "If your brother sins, rebuke him; and if he repents, forgive him. And if he sins against you seven times a day, and returns to you seven times, saying, 'I repent,' forgive him." Certainly the disciples recognized how difficult Jesus' instruction was to live out, just as we do. In fact, many Christians struggle with issues of forgiveness every day. "Increase our faith!" the disciples implore in response (v. 5).

Although Jesus proceeded to talk about mustard seeds and mulberry trees, the disciples knew exactly what He meant. He wasn't really concerned with the seeds and trees at all—He was speaking about forgiveness. When someone wrongs us numerous times, we have an option: either we succumb to the roots of bitterness, or we renounce bitterness. Jesus said that in such moments, we don't need *more* faith—we simply need to *exercise the faith we have.* We can speak with covenant authority and say, "In Jesus' name I renounce a spirit of bitterness." Our verbal response has results because we speak with covenant authority. On the other hand, if we hold on to the offense, it becomes "spiritual cancer." But we don't have to do that. By exercising the authority that is ours, even though we have been wronged time and time again, we can refuse to be a recipient of bitterness. We can say, "By the authority of Jesus I refuse to let a spirit of bitterness come into my life. By the power given me by the authority of the covenant, I rebuke a spirit of bitterness. I will live a pleasant life; I choose to walk in peace."

we have the Spirit of God

Christians can make these kinds of choices and exercise this kind of authority because we are made in God's likeness. Genesis tells us that God said, "Let Us make man in Our image" (1:26). When God made us, He put a "piece" of His Spirit in us. Some argue that we're simply made from dust. While it is true that Gen. 2 states that the Lord formed man from dust, the scripture goes on to declare that "[God] breathed into his nostrils the breath of life; and man became a living being" (v. 7). We have the breath of God in us!

God created us to be covenant children. And although our bodies are made from dust, our spirits are made from God himself. 1 Cor. 2:12 says it this way, "Now we have received, *not* the spirit of the world, but *the Spirit who is from God,* so that we may know the things freely given to us by God" (emphasis added).

Let's briefly review these principles. God has all authority. He gave authority over the earth to Adam. Satan contested that authority, and Adam dropped the ball. Satan picked up the ball, and in so doing, all humanity was brought under the curse of sin. Rom. 6:16-18 says that we were then "slaves" under him. Humanity relinquished its authority, but it would be up to God to set a plan in motion to get it back—and that's exactly what He did.

review and reflect

1. List three areas in which you can apply the teaching of the covenant to your life.

2. Discuss the relationship between faith and authority.

3. How do believers exercise authority?

4. How have words shaped your life?

5. Discuss the jurisprudence of the universe.

9

reclaiming the authority of the COVENANT

∞

How would God reclaim for humanity the authority Adam so foolishly forfeited? God can't simply rip it out of the hands of Satan. Why not? Because He is a God of integrity. He keeps His word. He gave authority to humanity, and humanity could do with it what they wanted. Tragically, they released control to Satan.

Here's one way of understanding the scenario. After my father retired from farming in Kansas, he leased the farm to my cousin. For the sake of illustration, let's suppose my cousin planted wheat where we had always grown corn. If my father had insisted that my cousin return the land to corn, my cousin could have said, "Well, you may own the land, but I have the lease—I can do with this field what I want to."

Similarly, Adam had the "earth lease." The earth belonged to God, of course, but He had given Adam authority over its use. In turn, Adam (humanity) gave the authority over to Satan. Since man gave it up, only a Man—Jesus—could get it back.

Parity covenant – & equals   Suzerain – unequals

Not surprisingly, the provision for this is in the Abrahamic covenant. You'll recall that in God's covenant with Abraham, as in any covenant-making ceremony, the parties exchanged belongings. In the suzerain covenant (in which a king has everything and a peasant has nothing) the king says, "Everything I have belongs to you." The peasant says, "I have nothing to give except myself." In this case, God said, "I want you, Abraham. I want you, and I want your offspring."

God's plan—the abrahamic covenant

The result is that God gained "legal access" (in the jurisprudence of the universe) back into the human race, multigenerations later, by one named Mary, who was in the lineage of Abraham. She conceived as a virgin after being overshadowed by the Holy Spirit, and God put on earth a Man who is sinless. Jesus—fully Man, fully God—will be the One to reclaim or wrench back the authority from Satan.

mary's "seed"

Through the lineage of Abraham, God sets in motion His great plan of redemption, of restoration. Our first clue regarding this is found as early as Gen. 3:15, in which God is speaking to the serpent: "I will put enmity between you and the woman, and between your seed and her seed; he shall bruise you on the head, and you shall bruise him on the heel." Every other time we see "seed" (offspring) in Scripture, the reference is to "his" seed, that of the male. But this reference, "her" seed, refers to Mary, who will someday give birth to Jesus. "And between your seed" (God is talking to the serpent, or Satan, referring to demonic forces) and her seed there will be great strife. Mary's "seed," of course, is Jesus.[1] "He [Jesus] shall bruise you

[Satan] on the head." This means it will be a lethal blow. "And you [Satan] shall bruise him [Jesus] on the heel." You may injure Him and think you've driven Him to final death on the Cross, but you will not prevail. He will conquer the grave. He will rise from the dead.

mary's conception—the spoken word

God's covenant with Abraham means that everything Abraham has belongs to God—and that includes his offspring. God now reenters the human race through Mary, a descendant of Abraham. Luke 1:30-38 tells about the conversation between the angel and Mary:

The angel said to her "Do not be afraid, Mary; for you have found favor with God. And behold, you will conceive in your womb and bear a son, and you shall name Him Jesus. He will be great and will be called the Son of the Most High; and the Lord God will give Him the throne of His father David; and He will reign over the house of Jacob forever, and His kingdom will have no end."

Mary said to the angel, "How can this be, since I am a virgin?"

The angel answered and said to her, "The Holy Spirit will come upon you, and the power of the Most High will overshadow you; and for that reason the holy child shall be called the Son of God. And behold, even your relative Elizabeth has also conceived a son in her old age; and she who was called barren is now in her sixth month. For nothing will be impossible with God."

And Mary said, "Behold, the bondslave of the Lord; be it done to me according to your word." And the angel departed from her.

*But instead of resisting
these obvious complications
about to enter her life,
Mary conformed her heart
to the word and will of
God. "Be it done to me
according to your word,"
she said.*

Mary could have protested becoming pregnant out of wedlock in a small town, where everyone would notice. But instead of resisting these obvious complications about to enter her life, Mary conformed her heart to the word and will of God. "Be it done to me according to your word," she said. And I believe in that very moment Mary conceived. This is the essence of successful prayer.

What kind of faith is this? The same kind of faith Jesus described in Mark 11:23, "Truly I say to you, whoever *says* to this mountain, 'Be taken up and cast into the sea,' and does not doubt in his heart, but believes that what he says is going to happen, it will be granted him." Jesus wasn't into moving *literal* mountains any more than He was into uprooting mulberry trees. In the Jewish idiom, "mountains" meant difficulties, seemingly impossible situations. Mountain-moving faith says, "God, I know it is Your plan and Your desire for my marriage not to fail. So in the name of Jesus, by the authority of God, because we are covenant partners, I speak to the 'mountain' in my marriage: Marriage, be made whole. Be made well; be made complete."

the word became flesh   Moral authority

John 1:1-3, 14 says, "In the beginning was the Word, and the Word was with God, and the Word was God. He was in the beginning with God. All things came into being through Him, and apart from Him nothing came into being that has come into being. . . . *And the Word became flesh*" (emphasis added).

Find out what God's will is—His Word, His intent—and you cannot do that unless you're *saturated* with His Word. Soak your Spirit with *His* Word, link your tongue up, and speak *His* Word to the circumstances of life. Don't keep announcing the problem—God knows the problem—but instead, speak His Word to the circumstances of life, for you have been given authority.

Again, I believe that Mary experienced the power of the spoken word, conceiving the instant she declared her conformity with God's Word. And what did she do next? She went and announced to Elizabeth, "The Mighty One has done great things for me" (Luke 1:49). She knew this was so because she had received the Word—God's Word—into her spirit. This text provides a picture of how prayer works. As God's Word—God's will—comes to us, we receive it, declare it, and pray it. And then it begins to manifest in the physical, observable domain. That's what occurred in Genesis. God spoke, and the earth was created. Now He "enforces" His will through us—through people who pray in accordance with His will. And situations on earth are changed. Although the phrase "the Word became flesh" in John 1:14 refers exclusively to Jesus, the Word (will) of God is still becoming "flesh" (being evidenced in the physical world of the five senses) when we pray (assuming that we are praying His Word—His will).

zacharias—not speaking God's word

Not everyone responds to the voice of God with the faith of Mary. Earlier in Luke 1 we find another instance of the angel talking, this time in the Temple to Zacharias, Mary's cousin by marriage: "Do not be afraid, Zacharias, for your petition has been heard, and your wife Elizabeth will bear you a son, and you will give him the name John" (Luke 1:13).

Zacharias asked the angel, "How can I be sure of this? I'm an old man, and my wife is well along in years." Unlike Mary, he didn't ask how it would happen, which is an issue of curiosity and faith. Instead, he stated the reason that the pregnancy could not or should not occur. The result of his *un*faith is immediate. "And now you will not able to speak until the day this happens, because you did not believe my words, which will come true at their proper time."

Can you imagine the angel saying, "If we don't shut your mouth, we'll never get that miracle"?

When Zacharias left the Temple, he could not speak to the crowd that was waiting outside. They realized he had seen a vision, for he kept making signs to them but remained unable to speak. People who understand authority are careful about what they say!

Jesus vs. satan

For 700 years the prophets and those who followed them had decreed that One would be born of a virgin. Every time God does something profoundly important on earth, He gets people like you and me to decree it and declare it in conformity with His authority. That's why prayer is important. That's why speaking His Word is important.

Mary's obedience set the stage for the continuation of the cosmic struggle for authority. Through her, Jesus came to earth preparing to take authority from Satan. It was as if Jesus and Satan were political candidates, each with his own platform. Jesus describes both "platforms" in John 10:10, "The thief comes only to steal and kill and destroy; I came that they may have life, and have it abundantly." First John 3:8 is Jesus' "purpose statement": "The Son of God appeared for this purpose, to destroy the works of the devil."

In His very first sermon Jesus speaks in covenant language as He defines His mission: "THE SPIRIT OF THE LORD IS UPON ME, BECAUSE HE ANOINTED ME TO PREACH THE GOSPEL TO THE POOR," he says in Luke 4:18, quoting from Isaiah. "HE

HAS SENT ME TO PROCLAIM RELEASE TO THE CAPTIVES, AND RE-COVERY OF SIGHT TO THE BLIND, TO SET FREE THOSE WHO ARE OPPRESSED." This is His "agenda."

Jesus' proclamation is the backdrop for the cosmic struggle between Satan and Jesus. In Matthew, Mark, and Luke, we find militaristic language: the kingdom of darkness versus the kingdom of light—two kingdoms, one with a rightful king and another with a challenger to the throne. One will win, and one will lose.

battlefronts

The battle between Jesus and Satan rages in five arenas:

1. *The hearts of humanity.* When Jesus wins over the hearts of people, we call that *evangelism.*

2. *The physical body.* When Jesus touches the physical body, we call that *healing.*

3. *The emotions.* When Jesus sets us free, we call that *deliverance.*

4. *Weather patterns.* This is not an area we normally regard as a battleground; however, Luke 8:23-25 tells us about a storm that nearly shipwrecked a boat the disciples and Jesus were riding in. The disciples panicked and woke Jesus, who rebuked the storm. We know that whatever Jesus did was in accordance with His Father's will. If He stopped the storm, then God probably hadn't caused it. But why would the enemy try to sink the boat containing Jesus and His closest friends? When the boat landed on the coast, Jesus encountered numbers of demons, which He cast into a herd of swine. The enemy, it would seem, didn't want Jesus and the disciples to reach the coast and drive out those demons.

5. *Death.* Satan ushers in death; Jesus overcomes it and ushers in life. John 11 gives a fascinating look at how the Pharisees plotted to kill Jesus. While the Pharisees were scheming,

Jesus charged into Bethany, a village on the outskirts of Jerusalem, and raised Lazarus from the dead. The Pharisees just couldn't see that this Man was unstoppable; they didn't seem to understand that He had victory over death—the ultimate victory being the Resurrection.

Today the battle of the kingdoms rages on. It's not for physical turf. It's to see who will rule and reign.

suffering vs. sickness

As Christians, we're in the fray. Jesus says we're going to suffer for His name's sake. We will be persecuted and reviled, and people will say all manner of evil against us. We are called to participate in "the fellowship of His sufferings" (Phil. 3:10).

Without doubt, suffering is part of being a Christian, but we must not confuse suffering for Christ with sickness and disease. In Scripture, we never see Jesus saying, "Brother, I know you're sick and I'm really sorry, but My Father did this to teach you a lesson; since I'm in accordance with My Father's will, I cannot heal you." Jesus never responded like that. He was brokenhearted at the impact of sin and the sickness and disease that had been brought upon the earth (see Matt. 9:36). He anguished over what the enemy had done, so He brought healing wherever He went. Was there any sickness in the original Garden of Eden? No. Is there any sickness in heaven? No. God does not bring sickness and disease; they are not part of His kingdom. Well, then—who introduced sickness and disease on earth? Satan did. Therefore, sickness is not God's plan. It was—and still is—Satan's.

Then we may naturally ask, "What about godly Christians who are sick? Why aren't they *all* healed if it's God's desire for people to be well?" That is a superb question.[2] It appears that sickness can come from many sources: (1) *Our failure to care for ourselves.* For example, I recently had some surgery. I can't blame it on God *or* the devil. As much as I hate to admit it, I violated some basic principles of health, and I paid a price for it. Some sickness is brought on us by our own decisions. (2) *Simply living in a fallen world.* I like to refer to sickness from this source as having been *in*directly brought by Satan. It was Satan who brought pain, heartache, sickness, and death. That was not God's original dream, of course. The fall of Adam had horrific implications for every component of life—including our health. (3) *Direct action by Satan.* Simply put, some illness is a result of a direct frontal physical attack by the enemy. For example, Jesus says of the crippled woman He healed in Luke 13, "Satan has bound [her] for eighteen long years" (v. 16).

Notice that in the three above-mentioned sources for sickness, I did *not* say that *God* causes sickness. Why not? Because He doesn't. He's a wonderful, loving Heavenly Father. He loves His kids. I have four children. I don't want any of them to be sick, and if I had the power to lay sickness on them, I certainly wouldn't do it. Why not? Because I love them. If an earthly father loves like this, how much more does our Heavenly Father love us? "Every *good* thing . . . and every *perfect* gift is from above" (James 1:17, emphasis added).

"But wait a minute," you may say. "I know that God ministers profoundly when people are sick." That's true. All of us hear more clearly from God when we have faced difficult physical pain and illness. And God's presence is spectacular in times of suffering caused by a disease. But that still does *not* mean that *God sent* the disease.

In summary, don't confuse "suffering" with "sickness." Will we suffer for Christ? Yes! The Scriptures repeatedly tell us that we will suffer. In fact, the verse that God used to call me to the pastoral ministry states that "it has been granted for Christ's sake, not only to believe in Him, but also to suffer for His sake" (Phil. 1:29). However, suffering and sickness are not the same. If we're going to truly identify with the suffering of Jesus, we're going to have to do it some other way than through sickness, because He was never sick. But He did suffer. He went to the Cross. And He asks us to do the same.

"luck" vs. God's blessing

I recently heard of a couple being interviewed on television. "We don't know why *God caused* our child to be born deformed," they said. "But we were *lucky* and found a plastic surgeon to repair the damage" (emphasis added). Their approach would have been more biblical if they had said, "We don't understand why in the course of human events, in this broken world that has been ravaged and traumatized by the enemy, our child was born this way. But, praise God, in His wisdom He released medical knowledge on a group of surgeons. He gave us the ability to gain strength and wealth to be able to afford help, and He brought our paths together. And, thank God—we were able to find help." Do you see the difference? We hang sickness on God. Jesus never viewed it that way. He viewed it as a contested area. He brought health and healing everywhere He walked.

"fire truck syndrome"

Many church people suffer from what I call "fire truck syndrome." I grew up on a farm nine miles from our small town. As a child, I saw a fire truck only two times, and both times I noticed it was beside a house that was burning. I mistakenly assumed that firefighters on fire trucks must start fires, because they were always "at the scene of the crime."

This is what happens in church. Sometimes Satan comes

along and beats the living daylights out of somebody, and because God shows up with an amazing force of His presence, people assume that God did the damage.

The truth is that the enemy may bring horrible things, but God can turn them for good. The fire truck was there, but the fire truck didn't start the fire. I once heard of a man who said, "Well, God broke my leg. He knew I needed a rest, so He put me in the hospital for a month." What kind of a God would that be? If I did the same to my son, I'd be in jail for child abuse. If God committed half the atrocities He is accused of, He ought to be arrested! If He wants us to rest, He can put us in a cabin beside a lake. He doesn't need to break our legs to do it.

The enemy traumatizes us and brings wounding, heartache, and trauma. In the midst of that, God's presence comes. Due to God's presence, some people mistakenly assume that God *sent* the calamity. No, He ministers *in spite of* the tragedy, not *because of* it. If we want to know God's will about sickness and pain, let's look at what Jesus did. He's a "chip off the old block." He's the "spitting image of His Dad." Jesus was always in total conformity to His Father's will. And again, Jesus never once said, "I can't heal you, because My Father brought this on you." He brought healing, deliverance, and hope.

God's work vs. satan's work

Acts 10:38 tells us, "You know of Jesus of Nazareth, how God anointed Him with the Holy Spirit and with power, and how He went about doing good and healing all who were *oppressed by the devil,* for God was with Him" (emphasis added). Notice who is oppressing—the devil. But Jesus came "to destroy the works of the devil" (1 John 3:8).

Luke 13, which we looked at previously, demonstrates this truth profoundly. When Christ encountered the woman who was bent over and in great pain, He asked, "Who is this daughter of Abraham that she should be traumatized like this?" Daughter of Abraham? Abraham had been deceased for 2,000 years. Why was He referring to Abraham? Because she was part of the Abrahamic covenant. She was a "covenant child," yet she was in bondage to infirmity because Satan had oppressed her (Luke 13:16). In essence Jesus was saying, "Satan, who do you think you are, messing with one of the covenant kids? You have no right to do that. I put a stop to it!"

Jesus came to set the captives free!

Prayer: *Father, help us learn to live in the power of the covenant, knowing that You've come to set us free.*

review and reflect

1. How will God reclaim the authority Adam forfeited?

2. How does the story of Mary's faith apply to us today?

3. What are the five arenas of battle?

4. List the arenas of battle in your life.

10

ruling and reigning in accordance with the COVENANT

∞

The battle rages throughout the ages—Jesus versus Satan. Although we should not underestimate our enemy, we should not give him too much credit either. Satan is *not* all-knowing. He is *not* omnipotent—all-powerful. He is *not* omnipresent. God alone has those qualities.

satan's ignorance

In Scripture it seems that Satan underestimates Jesus, seeming not to understand fully who He is. Jesus is a puzzle to the demonic forces—they understand His *divinity,* but it seems they cannot comprehend His full *humanity.* They accept the fact that He is *God,* but they challenge the fact that He is *man.* The demons appear to be confused.

In Luke 4 we see a demon crying out through a human being: "What business do we have with each other, Jesus of Nazareth? Have You come to destroy us? I know who You are— *the Holy One of God!*" (v. 34, emphasis added). This passage is especially interesting because early in His ministry Jesus didn't tell people who He was. Even His best friends didn't know. In fact, He didn't talk openly about His identity until well over halfway through His three-and-one-half-year ministry. But the demons knew, and they blurted out the information. "What are You doing here, God?" they exclaimed. Yet, despite this knowledge they still didn't seem to understand this One who is not the *son of Adam* (under the curse of sin), but the *Seed of Abraham* (totally sinless, thus *not* under their direction).[1]

the importance of Jesus' humanity

Jesus' humanity gave Him *legal* standing to be on earth (it was created for humanity), and consequently the right to win back the authority Adam lost. In Matt. 8:28-29, the demons are again confused about His humanity: "When He came to the other side into the country of the Gadarenes, two men who were demon-possessed met Him as they were coming out of the tombs. They were so extremely violent that no one could pass by that way. And they cried out, saying, 'What business do we have with each other, *Son of God?* Have You come here to torment us *before the time?*'" (emphasis added).

Once again, the demons understood that Jesus was fully the Son of God, but they did *not* seem to understand that He was also fully human, legally (rightfully) occupying earth, and was about to wrench back the authority that humanity—Adam— had surrendered. Though they were aware that at some point they would be destroyed—"Have You come here to torment us *before the time?*"—they taunted Jesus for coming when He did.

In Mark 5:6-7 we see a similar scenario: "Seeing Jesus from a distance, he ran up and bowed down before Him; and shouting with a loud voice, he said, 'What business do we have with each other, Jesus, *Son of the Most High God?* I *implore* You *by*

Most believers don't

understand the nature of

Jesus. We can't grasp the

fact that He was fully

human, that he had to be

fully human in order to

break the curse of Adam's

sin; that to break the curse,

Jesus had to be just like us.

God, do not torment me!'" (emphasis added). What we have here is a demon shrieking for God's help.

Since when did demons get the idea that they could appeal to God to get Jesus off their backs? But that's precisely what happens in this text. The word "implore" is a military term. Some translations use "adjure." The meaning of what the demon is saying is "I command you. I command you, by the authority of God: stop tormenting me." This demon has the audacity to appeal to God to get Jesus to stop tormenting him. Why? This demon knows he has the right to be here, because Adam handed control over to the devil and his hosts long ago when he sinned. But this demon doesn't grasp who Jesus really is. A man's (Adam's) sin gave them (the demons) power; it would take another Man to get it back. This demon cannot comprehend that Jesus could be fully *man* without ever coming under the control of Satan, that He could be absolutely sinless —that He could resist every temptation. Jesus never thought a wrong thought, spoke a wrong word, or was ever out of conformity with God's will. This One who is fully Man, yet sinless, prevails over the demonic hosts.

Most believers don't understand the nature of Jesus. We can't grasp the fact that He was fully human, that he *had* to be fully human to break the curse of Adam's sin; that to break the curse, Jesus had to be just like us. John 5:26-27 confirms this: "For just as the Father has life in Himself, even so He gave to the Son also to have life in Himself; and He [God the Father] gave Him authority to execute judgment, because He is the Son of *Man*" (emphasis added). Yes, Jesus is fully God, but for our sakes He is also fully human, yet sinless.

theories of the atonement

Jesus wins, and Satan is defeated; it's the story of the Cross.

When He died on the

Cross, He died spotless, and

at that point Satan became

a murderer and thus

committed himself to

"death row."

So how does the death and resurrection of this God-Man touch our lives today? As we look at the Cross, we can study the five or six theories of atonement. We can consider the Cross from various vantage points and come away with different understandings of exactly what happened. While most of these theories are probably valid interpretations, we'll consider just one that is especially relevant to covenant.

satan on death row

In this view of the Atonement, Jesus was pressed to the Cross by a murderous scheme of Satan. Just one week before, He had come into town a hero. On Palm Sunday the crowd had laid down branches saying, "Blessed is He who comes in the name of the Lord! Hosanna! Hosanna!" But then a few days later the crowd turned into a murderous mob screaming, "Kill Him!" Satan had incited the crowds and ignited the fury of the Roman leaders, so they executed the One who knew no sin. The threat to Satan's reign was over—or so he thought.

When Jesus died, He did not have any personal sin for which He was dying. He was dying as an innocent man—completely spotless, completely sinless. Not once was He out of alignment with the perfect will of the Father, and though He was enormously tempted, He was successful against it and therefore never came under Satan's control. So when He died on the Cross, He died spotless, and at that point Satan became a murderer and thus committed himself to "death row." He knew he was defeated. Innocent blood was shed, the provision for sin had been met, and Satan had sealed his own demise.

The impact of Jesus' death is emphasized in Heb. 2:14, which says, "Since then the children share in flesh and blood, He Himself [Jesus] likewise also partook of the same [became a man like us], that through death [Jesus' death] He might render powerless [strip away all the authority of] him who had the power of death, that is, the devil."

Col. 2:14-15 confirms the power of Jesus' death on the Cross: "Having canceled out the certificate of debt consisting of decrees against us, which was hostile to us; and He [Jesus] has taken it out of the way, having nailed it to the cross. When He had disarmed [stripped of all authority] the rulers and authorities [Satan and his demonic kingdom], He made a public display of them, having triumphed over them through Him." In Christ's death, the provision for Adam's sin and ours had been met.

satan's presumed power

If Jesus won at the Cross, why does Satan give believers so much trouble today? If he was defeated, why does he seem to have so much power? If you're a student of World War II, you'll remember the gap between D-Day and V-Day. The United States' participation in the European theater of war stretched over a span of approximately four years, from 1941 to 1945. V-Day signified the end of the war, when the Allied Forces, including the United States, were victorious. The enemy surrendered. But about a year before that, there was D-Day. On D-Day it became obvious that the Allied Forces would prevail. Germany had been crushed and would not win the war. Despite the certain defeat, Germany made one last attempt. During that one-year span there were more Allied casualties than in all the rest of the war put together.

Spiritually, we are between D-Day and V-Day. Satan knows he has been defeated, but until we get to V-Day, when the enemy will be finally destroyed, he is staging one last all-out attack.

We're in the interim now, and Satan is wreaking havoc on earth. But how could one who was stripped of his power seem to have so much strength? Here's a way to illustrate the answer to this question: Picture a bank robber who pulls a gun on a security guard in the bank. "Reach for the sky!" the robber says. Who has the *authority* and who has the *power* in this situation? The security guard has the authority, because he wears the badge. But he doesn't have the power—because someone else is holding the gun. But as time passes, the security guard looks closely at the gun and sees that, though it looks real, it's actually a child's toy pistol. At that point he pulls for his own gun. Now who has the power? He who has the authority (the badge) now has the power (the gun). But until the security guard discovered that the robber's pistol was only a toy, he was controlled by fear and deception.

our authority and our power

Many Christians are like the security guard. We know we have authority over the earth, because God gave it to us. But the enemy comes in with what looks real but isn't (like the toy gun) and rules by fear and deception. Too many times he pulls the gun on us, and we reach for the air, dropping our weapons. In that situation, although we have the authority, we lack the power. We need to realize that Satan's power is counterfeit. Ours is real. We have the authority (legal right) to be here on earth, and we should use the power God has given us.

ruling and reigning

Jesus gave authority to the Church. Why? According to a well-known confession of faith, the Westminster Shorter Catechism, our chief end (purpose) on earth is "to glorify God and enjoy him forever." Amazingly, the God of the universe desires a relationship with us. But that's not the only reason He gives us authority.

the climax of history

All of history is heading toward one great culmination, the Marriage Supper of the Lamb, that grand climax of time and eternity in which the Church will become the Bride of the Lamb, the Bride of Christ. When that happens, the Bride, according to the scripture, becomes a co-sovereign, co-eternal ruler with Christ. In the meantime, we have to learn how to rule and reign.

Paul Billheimer's *Destined for the Throne* describes it this way:

1. The earth was created to provide a suitable habitation for the human race.

2. The Messiah came for only one purpose—to give birth to His Church.

3. History is headed for one grand climax. The culmination of history is the Marriage Supper of the Lamb.

4. The Church will be "the bride, the wife of the Lamb," according to Rev. 21:9. The Church will be the eternal companion of Jesus. Eph. 5:25, 32 says it this way: "Husbands, love your wives, just as Christ also loved the church and gave Himself up for her. . . . This mystery is great; but I am speaking with reference to Christ and the church."

5. After the wedding, the Bride will be His eternal companion who will sit with Him on the throne . . . and will rule and reign with Him.

    1 Cor. 6:2-3 says, "Do you not know that the saints will judge the world? . . . Do you not know that we will judge angels?"

    2 Tim. 2:12 says, "If we endure, we will also reign with Him."

In Rev. 2:26 Jesus says, "He who overcomes, and he who keeps My deeds until the end, TO HIM I WILL GIVE AUTHORITY OVER THE NATIONS."

In Rev. 3:21 Jesus says, "He who overcomes, I will grant to him to sit down with Me on My throne, as I also overcame and sat down with My Father on His throne."

Rev. 5:10 confirms, "They will reign upon the earth."

6. We must be prepared for ruling and reigning. When you "marry into royalty," you have to be prepared for this queenly role. God has provided "on-the-job training." It is called *prayer.*

7. If the Church will not pray, God will not act. God will not go "over the head" of His Church to enforce His decisions.

8. Through prayer you are an enforcer of heaven's will . . . on earth. You are implementing His decisions here. Through prayer you have been given authority and administrative responsibilities for earthly events.[2]

Notice how often the phrase "on earth" appears in Matt. 16:19 and 18:18-19.

Matt. 16:19 (emphasis added)

"Whatever you bind on *earth*"

"Whatever you loose on *earth*"

Matt. 18:18-19 (emphasis added)

"Whatever you bind on *earth*"

"Whatever you loose on *earth*"

"If two of you agree on *earth*"

our power: prayer

Paul Billheimer wrote, "Heaven holds the key by which decisions governing earthly affairs are made, but we are the key by which these decisions are implemented. . . . Prayer is not over-coming reluctance in God. It is not persuading Him to do some-thing He is unwilling to do. It is implementing His decision."[3]

Many Christians have an inadequate view of prayer. We look toward God, pleading for Him to do that which we secret-ly believe He is unwilling to do. In reality, God wants us to speak that which is in conformity with His Word, His Will, and His Way. He wants us to bind and loose that which He has already declared to be bound and loosed in heaven. Simply put, *He's on our team (or we're on His)! He's cheering for us!*

This is why we pray, "Your Kingdom come, Your will be done on earth, just as it is up in heaven." It is not effectual to beg God to do things He has already committed to do. We see in Scripture that every time God does something on earth, He gets humans to agree and declare it and decree it—sometimes centuries before it actually takes place. Remember that Isaiah, speaking 700 years before Christ, decreed that a baby would be born of a virgin. He spoke in conformity with God's word, and it happened!

too busy to pray

Billheimer has an answer for those of us who protest we are too busy to pray:

> Too busy watching television, following sports, hunting, fishing, swimming, boating, engaging in farming or business, moonlighting. We are so busy with the cares and pleasures of this life trying to keep with the trend in new cars, new homes, new appliances, new furniture, etc., that we do not have time to pray. Someone has described a modern Ameri-can as a person who drives a bank-financed car over a bond-financed highway on credit card gas to open a charge account at a department store so he can fill his Savings and Loan-fi-

nanced home with installment-purchased furniture. May this not also be a description of many modern professed Christians? And may this not be one reason why modern Christians have so little time to pray?

If you can buy the new car, the new home, the new furniture, the new gadgets, hold down two jobs, and so on for the glory of God, well and good. But if we didn't have to have such a high standard of living, would we not have more time to pray? If we were not so intoxicated with travel, pleasure, vacations, and recreation, would we not have more time to pray? If we were not so enamored of sports and entertainment, would we not have more time to pray? We have more leisure than ever before—but less time to pray. We are not only cheating God and the world, but we are cheating ourselves. By our failure to pray, we are frustrating God's high purpose in the ages. We are robbing the world of God's best plan for it, and we are limiting our rank in eternity.[4]

seeing what the Father is doing

The key to effective prayer, to operating in His kind of power and authority, is to stay tuned-in to the Father. We don't pray for things that are out of conformity with God's will; instead we find out what the Father is doing, and like Jesus, we become one in accord with Him.

The key to knowing God's will is to see what He's doing. In John 5:19 Jesus says, "I say to you, the Son can do nothing of Himself, unless it is something He sees the Father doing." This idea is repeated four more times in this same Gospel: "I can do nothing on My own initiative" (5:30); "I can do nothing on My own initiative, but I speak these things as the Father taught Me" (8:28); "For I did not speak on My own initiative"

Backing me up

The key to knowing God's

will is to see what

He's doing.

(12:49); "I do not speak on My own initiative, but the Father abiding in Me does His works" (14:10). What Jesus is saying in these five verses is, "I don't do what I do on My own. I look and see what the Father is doing. I know His will, His word, His way. I speak it. I act on it." This simple strategy of Jesus is to be *our* "game plan" as well. Let's see what the Father desires to initiate, and then decree (pray) it.

kingdom, come!

Every time we pray the Lord's Prayer, we declare, "Kingdom, come! Will of God, be done!"

What is the Kingdom we pray for? "Kingdom" here means God's rule and reign. It means Jesus' rule and reign. We aren't supposed to timidly ask, "Kingdom, would you like to come? Will of God, would you like to be done?" No—we are to boldly declare, "Kingdom, come! Will of God, be done!" Where? On earth, just as it is in heaven. Jesus has given us keys to the Kingdom, and we have the authority to pray onto earth heaven's will.

When we pray, the Kingdom comes, manifested in healing and deliverance, as Matt. 9:35 declares. The same theme is repeated in Matt. 10:7-8 and 12:28. It appears again in Luke 10:9 when Jesus tells the 70 young believers that "if people wonder why they were healed from sickness, just tell them that they got a little too close to the Kingdom!" (author's paraphrase).

But the Kingdom's manifestations are more than healing and deliverance. When the Kingdom comes, there's a flurry of evangelistic fruit as hearts are moved from wickedness toward the Cross. When the Kingdom comes, hearts are drawn to righteousness, to holiness, to sanctification. When the Kingdom comes, there is deep concern for the poor, the downtrodden, and the impoverished (Luke 4:18). When the Kingdom comes, there is an outbreak of peace and joy. Simply put, amazing things happen when the Kingdom comes. And that's what we're praying and decreeing when we say, "Kingdom, come!"

a prayer for us all

Paul prays for us in Eph. 1:18-20 to grasp the implications of our covenant relationship. Notice the covenant language: "I pray that the eyes of your heart may be enlightened, so that you may know what is the hope of His calling, what are the riches of the glory of *His* inheritance [the swapping of assets is the inheritance] in the saints, and what is the surpassing greatness of *His* power [the exchange of power, and authority, and strengths] toward us who believe. These are in accordance with the working of the strength of *His* might [the exchange of strengths] which He brought about in Christ, when He raised Him from the dead, and seated Him at His right hand in the heavenly places." Simply stated, such promises are for all of us and we can look forward to receiving them.

timing

The covenant promises are not invalidated if they are slow in coming. I agree with the one who said, "God may never be late, but He certainly misses all the good opportunities to be early!" Sometimes a covenant promise comes long after we have prayed it, spoken it, or decreed it. In Josh. 1 we see the Israelites entering into the Promised Land. Let us not forget that the fulfillment of the promise was 600 years after the promise was made. Long before, the Lord made a covenant with Abram, saying, "I'm giving you the land." For 400 years the Israelites were slaves in a lonely land. Another 200 years is not

Speaking the covenant

even referenced in this biblical narrative. It was 600 years between the time the promise was made and the time the people entered the Promised Land, described in Josh. 1.

The fact that there is a long duration does not diminish our confidence in the covenant. The covenant is never invalidated by virtue of taking a long time to fulfill. In the meantime, Christians are to live in power and authority without fear; it is our privilege to rule and reign in the kingdom of God.

the covenant—final thoughts

H. Clay Trumbull, in his turn-of-the-century "earth-shattering" work on the covenant, cited an elderly missionary from Philadelphia by the name of R. M. Luther. Luther had been a missionary among the Karens in Burma. Luther had seen covenant making for many years and made this amazing statement: "I have never heard of the blood covenant being broken. . . . The way in which the blood covenant was spoken of always implied that its rupture was an unheard-of thing."[5]

Let me close this book by saying that I have never heard of the covenant being kept by any human; but on the part of God the Father and on the part of His Son Jesus Christ, *I have never heard of the covenant being broken.* The covenant was not merely made—it was *kept* for you and for me, and we enjoy the inexplicable benefits of it.

Prayer: *Our God and our Father, thank You for Your Word and Your comfort. In Jesus' name. Amen.*

review and reflect

1. Why did Satan have trouble accepting Jesus' humanity?

2. Discuss the Lord's Prayer in light of the truth of the covenant.

3. How did Jesus seal the demise of Satan?

4. What is the key to knowing God's will?

NOTES

Chapter 1

1. Robert E. Coleman, *The New Covenant* (Deerfield, Ill.: Christian Outreach, 1984), 86.

2. H. Clay Trumbull, *The Blood Covenant* (1893; reprint, Kirkwood, Mo.: Imprint Books, 1975), 297.

3. Ibid., 263-64, emphasis added.

4. For a concise study of the covenants, see Charles Gilbert Weston, *The Seven Covenants: A Study of the Bible Through the Seven Covenants of the Scriptures* (Jefferson, Oreg.: Weston Bible Ministries, 1990).

Chapter 2

1. See Duane Weis, *Paid for in Blood* (Dallas: self-published, n.d.), 58.

2. Al Truesdale and Bonnie Perry, *A Dangerous Hope: Encountering the God of Hope* (Kansas City: Beacon Hill Press of Kansas City, 1997), 27.

3. Bob Phillips, *Covenant: Its Blessings—Its Curses* (Lindale, Tex.: World Challenge, 1986), 9.

4. E. W. Kenyon, *The Blood Covenant* (n.p.: Gospel Publishing Society, 1997), 12.

5. Coleman, *The New Covenant,* 86.

6. Weis, *Paid for in Blood,* 111-12.

7. Ibid., 112. Also see Phillips, *Covenant,* 11.

Chapter 3

1. Weis, *Paid for in Blood,* 31.

Chapter 4

1. For a much fuller discussion of this profound event, see Andrew Murray, *The Two Covenants* (Fort Washington, Pa.: Christian Literature Crusade, 1995), chapters 9—11.

2. This veil split in spite of its massive thickness and size. According to Alfred Eideersheim, *The Life and Times of Jesus the Messiah,* Book 5 (McLean, Va.: MacDonald Publishing Co., n.d.), 611, "The veils before the Most Holy Place were 40 cubits (60 feet) long, and 20 cubits (30 feet) wide, of the thickness of the palm of the hand. . . . In the exaggerated language of the time, it needed 300 priests to manipulate each."

Chapter 5

1. Truesdale and Perry, *A Dangerous Hope,* 27.

2. Weis, *Paid for in Blood,* 100. See also Phillips, *Covenant,* 11.

3. *Paid for in Blood,* 103.

4. Ibid.

5. For a further discussion of the suzerain (or vassal) covenants, see Meredith G. Kline, *Treaty of the Great King: The Covenant Structure of Deuteronomy* (Grand Rapids: Wm. B. Eerdmans, 1963), 13 ff. Also see Truesdale and Perry, *A Dangerous Hope,* 26.

6. According to David Alsebrook, *The Precious Blood* (Brentwood, Tenn.: Sure Word Ministries, 1979), 159, "It cannot be said, in all honesty, that a parity . . . could possibly exist in a covenant between the divine and the human."

Chapter 6

1. Kenyon, *The Blood Covenant,* 6, 12-13.

2. Trumbull, *The Blood Covenant,* 318.

Chapter 7

1. Trumbull, *The Blood Covenant,* 265-66.

2. It speaks mercy. See H. A. Maxwell Whyte, *The Power of the Blood* (New Kensington, Pa.: Whitaker House, 1973), 31.

Chapter 9

1. "Only Jesus is called the seed of a woman," according to M. R. DeHaan, *The Chemistry of the Blood* (Grand Rapids: Zondervan, 1943), 25.

2. For a detailed look at that question, see the extensive outline and eight-tape series "Understanding Healing," by James L. Garlow, available from Skyline Wesleyan Church of Rancho San Diego, 11330 Hwy. 94, La Mesa, CA 91941. Telephone: 619-660-5000.

Chapter 10

1. See DeHaan, *The Chemistry of the Blood,* 25.

2. Adapted from Paul E. Billheimer, *Destined for the Throne* (Fort Washington, Pa.: Christian Literature Crusade, 1975), 22-23, 25-27, 48-50. Used by permission of Bethany House Publishers, 11400 Hampshire Ave. S., Minneapolis, MN 55438.

3. Ibid., 51-52.

4. Ibid., 52-53.

5. Trumbull, *The Blood Covenant,* 314.